Songs of Other Places

NEW WRITING SCOTLAND 32

Edited by
Gerry Cambridge
and
Zoë Strachan

Gaelic adviser:
Rody Gorman

Association for Scottish Literary Studies

Association for Scottish Literary Studies
Scottish Literature, 7 University Gardens
University of Glasgow, Glasgow G12 8QH
www.asls.org.uk

ASLS is a registered charity no. SC006535

First published 2014

British Library Cataloguing in Publication Data

A CIP record for this book is available
from the British Library

ISBN 978-1-906841-19-5

The Association for Scottish Literary Studies
acknowledges the support of Creative Scotland
towards the publication of this book

ALBA | CHRUTHACHAIL

Printed by Bell & Bain Ltd, Glasgow

CONTENTS

INTRODUCTION

This is my first year of three as an editor for *New Writing Scotland*, and Zoë Strachan's final year. She had suggested a poet as editor to balance her own knowledge of prose. Similarly, I was a touch nervy about the business of selecting fiction for this anthology. Would the fact that I've never written any myself mean my choices would be less informed? (Fiction is different from other types of prose, of course: I hope I am well enough able to bring a clear eye to the latter.)

As it happened, there was a surprising amount of overlap in taste between our selections for this year's *New Writing Scotland*, and where there was any doubt on my part, fiction-wise, I was happy to consult Zoë for guidance. Perhaps some elements of good writing – among them, clarity, authority, confidence of execution, an individual way of looking and sufficient technical panache to fulfil that vision – are universal.

This is a national anthology which has an international reach. It follows that the bar for acceptance should be a high one. My instinct as an editor is partly for stringence and toughness. These sound boring qualities, of course, and perhaps they are, but with luck they produce something which is more reader- than writer-friendly. I dislike anthologies which force readers to become their own editors. You want a high 'hit rate', and I see *New Writing Scotland* as, hopefully, a showcase for 'the best' – something, for instance, that the so-called ordinary reader might go through for pleasure. In my view, when one is confident of that 'hit rate', it's possible to take chances on some selections – the reader will come with you. This allows space in such an anthology for that adventurousness which is a part of the creative act itself. But only within limits, mind. Too much, and the eyebrow is raised and the red pen out.

None of which of course should be visible to the reader: only that freshness of new, original work which intrigues, engages, moves, or makes some clarifying pattern out of that dazzling chaos which surrounds us every day.

Gerry Cambridge

Even as an adult, I enjoy a spot of rockpooling. Shifting stones, parting seaweed, scooping sand. Picturesque at times, precarious and slippery at others, progress punctuated by the shock of a scuttling hermit crab, the wavering bloom of a sea anemone. My three-year term editing *New Writing Scotland* is over and I am left with a sense of having rockpooled through Scotland's psyche, glimpsing memories of the past and projections for the future, secrets and obsessions, fears and passions. It has been hard work, but a privilege. All writers are nosy, all writers like reading.

What have I learned? Scottish writers can be found all over the world, and writers from all over the world can be found in Scotland. Their concerns are not parochial. This year writers were far more inspired by situations around the globe than by the very big question that will be asked at home, shortly after this volume appears. Scottish writers have a passion for genre, and adopt and subvert its conventions with gusto. They're more wary of formal experimentation, but when they embrace it, the results can be dazzling. The standard of submissions has increased over the past three years, and we're receiving more – and better – poetry than ever before.

These are generalisations, of course. Both editors read every submission on its own terms, and for its own merit. It takes us a long time to make decisions because Scottish writers are prolific, and more of them are submitting work to *New Writing Scotland* than ever before. My house was colonised by piles of manuscripts for months at a time. The volume cannot hold every piece that might merit inclusion, and so our final decisions are tough. We lay aside pieces that we've enjoyed enormously, or that have moved us deeply. And we give you, our reader, the treasures that we've found. I hope that some of these songs from other places will shine for you as well.

Zoë Strachan

NEW WRITING SCOTLAND 33: SUBMISSION INSTRUCTIONS

The thirty-third volume of *New Writing Scotland* will be published in summer 2015. Submissions are invited from writers resident in Scotland or Scots by birth, upbringing or inclination. All forms of writing are welcome: autobiography and memoirs; creative responses to events and experiences; drama; graphic artwork (monochrome only); poetry; political and cultural commentary and satire; short fiction; travel writing or any other creative prose may be submitted, but not full-length plays or novels, though self-contained extracts are acceptable. The work must not be previously published, submitted, or accepted for publication elsewhere, and may be in any of the languages of Scotland.

Submissions should be typed on one side of the paper only and the sheets secured at the top left corner. Prose pieces should be double-spaced and carry an approximate word-count. **You should provide a covering letter, clearly marked with your name and address.** *Please also put your name on the individual works.* If you would like to receive an acknowledgement of receipt of your manuscript, please enclose a stamped addressed postcard. If you would like to be informed if your submission is unsuccessful, or would like your submissions returned, you should enclose a stamped addressed envelope with sufficient postage. Submissions should be sent by **30 September 2014**, in an A4 envelope, to the address below. We are sorry but we cannot accept submissions by fax or email.

Please be aware that we have limited space in each edition, and therefore shorter pieces are more suitable – although longer items of exceptional quality may still be included. **Please send no more than four poems, or one prose work.** Successful contributors will be paid at the rate of £20 per published page. Authors retain all rights to their work(s), and are free to submit and/or publish the same work(s) elsewhere after they appear in *New Writing Scotland*.

ASLS
Scottish Literature
7 University Gardens
University of Glasgow
Glasgow G12 8QH, Scotland

Tel +44 (0)141 330 5309
www.asls.org.uk

Gregor Addison

CHICAGO, 1930s

Those who came before us, whose feet once trod
the snow-shod sidewalks of a Chicago night,
its neon glow, its gangster whitewalls, who turned
from their fishing towns and farms with wide-eyed
but predatory anticipation
to eke out a life in service, to shift
the beat of their country steps; we rearrange
the accent of their footfalls. Here, I sift
old photographs, shake them, waiting for gold
to fall into my lap. Only the cold
Thirties winter is intelligible,
the rest is re-runs, half-truths, lies, passable
as hand-me-downs slurred over drinks. The line
of their reason staggered now to match my own.

CO-ORDINATES

You stuffed leaves in a tin, the thin stained sheets
that weathered wartime upheaval to fall
into other's hands, the loose co-ordinates

of where you'd been, a paper-trail of all
the passages packed into a life off land.
For forty years you gathered in a trawl

of foreign parts, of far-off ports, deck-hand,
master, a far-cry from a farm in Arbroath.
In Bridgeton, the children at the close-mouth scanned

the street's horizon, checked trams, stepping aboard
to study strangers' faces, and kept a record
like loose cuttings from a life mapped out abroad.

Claire Askew

THE HEART

is a marshmallow, punctured
and stuck in a fire. Sparks
spit-fleck the grey shale beach
and the grey shale beach
tightens and loosens the lake.
The heart shimmies off
its sugar coat. It's skinned,
glittering like a windpipe.
The vexed sun falls into the valley.

The trick is knowing
when to pull back.
Hold still through the drip
and ooze, watch it crisp, sick
of its own sweetness. Then draw it
into the hard air to suck off
the crust. The bruise
of the lake will darken. The heart
will get over you:

gunking your fingernails,
scalding the roof of your mouth
like a hot coin. But better
this sweet mess, the embers
guttering down. Hold it
too long in the flame
and the heart catches,
the stick catches,
then you,

gooseflesh and tallow,
kindling of buttons and wool.
And the beach catches, and the trees
with their long teeth in the lake.
The moon gets up and rolls
its cold eye as you burn down
your whole small world.
The moon has seen this
many times before.

Paul Brownsey

THE PLACE OF RELIGION IN MODERN THOUGHT

'The eyes – they're all you can see of it.'

Because of the frenzied barking that crashes upon them from cages and coops all along the open shed, Jamie has to lean close to Alex to make himself heard, though he's careful not to lean too close. In darkness behind a grille, white orbs flash rhythmically, openings for disorder threatening the whole world.

Jamie continues, 'Look how it's leaping up-down, up-down, like clockwork. That dog has been driven *mad*.'

'So you've become an expert on mental illness in dogs since you've been on your own.' Anxiety caused Jamie to hear Alex easily above the barrage. Beneath the barking there are thumps and bangs as dogs hurl themselves against walls or wire. They're penned singly or in pairs.

Jamie wants to say, 'Been on my own, have I?' but in fact says, 'I don't think we speak of mental *illness* these days. We are supposed to say mental health *problems*.'

Sod it, he's fallen back into the sort of teasing challenge that marked so many of their old conversations. But it's comforting, like giving yourself a meal you remember from childhood, a boiled egg with fingers of buttered bread.

The dogs' noise is still going on even now that the track has brought Alex and Jamie to the benevolent double-dormered farmhouse, stone-built, honeyed in the morning sunshine, *1731* carved in the door lintel. There's no-one about, which relieves Jamie of the business of asking permission to go through the farm to get onto the hill. He needs the energy for a very different confrontation that's been brewing ever since his ex-, if a man of forty-eight can talk of having an ex-, phoned out of the blue to suggest going for a hike.

But for the moment Jamie just adds, 'No, not *problems*. Mental health *issues*. Everything these days is an *issue*. Doctors don't deal with health *matters*, they deal with health *issues*. Why do we speak as if everything is a matter of dispute?'

Yes, the cue still works. Alex embarks on one of his lectures on the social and political implications of language. 'Once there was a presumption that everyone had essentially the same feelings, so we have words like 'charming', which means that it's likely to charm *everyone*. But now we have the opposite presumption, that people vary enormously in their sentiments and tastes, so we assume that everything is a matter of dispute, an *issue*.' But then he laughs in a way that he never did after his homilies of old. He turns to look at the view, walking backwards.

Below them is a panorama of peace and blessing: newly green fields, ewes and lambs in profusion, the sun in a high blue sky expanding the heart with a message of the kindness of nature.

'It's so All-in-the-April-Evening. I thooooouuuuuuuught of the Laaaaamb of Gaaaawwwwwddd.' Jamie parodies the mincing diction of a pious singer of the song. The renewal of the earth in spring has to be an omen that Alex's love, too, is being renewed. Jamie says, 'It's bloody cruel, those dogs cooped up.'

'Oh, they'll get let out in due course. Plenty of sheep to work on.' Alex still has his irritating omniscience, but the *Guardian*-reading concerned-citizen Alex that Jamie lived with for nineteen years wouldn't have been so dismissive of cruelty.

'But you were the good works one, taking stands. Dragging me to work in the women's refuge shop. Sending me out with your Iraq War leaflets. Don't dogs matter?' They're now well above the domestic huddle of the farmhouse and its outbuildings. 'I'd love a dog. The love. The love people want from God, a dog's love. The devotion.' He doesn't quite manage, 'A dog doesn't leave you.' He springs in a very carefree manner over a gate, and fields are left behind for open hillside.

'Without my fastidiousness about dog hairs everywhere, you could have got yourself one.' *Could have got yourself*, not *Can get yourself*: does that carry a stronger implication that Alex means their separation is over?

'Out at work all day, how can I leave a dog by itself?' And Jamie's missed his footing and toppled full-length into the heather, releasing a warm cloud of sweetness that embraces them both. His 'Fuck!', while natural enough at the tumble, is really about the fact that he's given away the state of his love-life, if someone of forty-eight can use that phrase; given away his domestic arrangements, anyway. He springs up immediately so that Alex won't think he's lying there waiting for Alex's arms to help him up. He says, 'A dog doesn't leave you.'

But it's too nice a day for ill humour. Sunshine kindles faith that it will end in joy greater than which none can be imagined. After all, what goes around comes around, you get what you deserve in life, and Jamie did nothing to deserve being dumped. They walk on in comfortable talk about safe topics like idiocies at their workplaces and Alex's nieces and nephews, all of whom Jamie mentions by name like someone displaying qualifications.

Then they're too hot for talk and it's too steep. They've gone separate ways to skirt peat hags. Alex, nimble and fast despite his stocky build, is some way off, ascending by a different shoulder from the one Jamie is puffing up. But they'll reunite at the summit – it's a symbol, Jamie is being shown something! For a moment Jamie sinks into the comfort of that thought, then says 'For fuck's sake!' out loud to a bee nuzzling the heather.

At the breezy summit there's a big grin to welcome them. Someone has stuck a thick fence-post into the cairn and carved a face in it, crude yet skilful. They sit against the cairn and eat the sandwiches each made for himself, Jamie having feared it would be tempting fate to offer to make sandwiches for them both. The universe would have punished such presumption by causing Alex, at the end of the day, to say only, 'Well, we must stay in touch.'

After a while Jamie wriggles flat and now he's lulled beneath the breeze and the high rhapsody of larks in an invisible layer of pure warmth and pure peace. The earth breathes goodness; its scents evoke salad and cricket bats. The face in the fence-post, upside-down to Jamie, smiles a blessing on him, and on Alex, and, yes, on the pair of them.

'Christ, listen!' Jamie sits up. 'Can't you hear them? Up here, even. The dogs. Miles away. You can't even see the farm.'

'Have you forgotten I'm a little hard of hearing?' He still doesn't trim his ear hair.

'I can hear them, I tell you. Still locked up. Someone should do something. Report the farmer.'

'Jamie, it's nothing to do with you. Not your responsibility. Vengeance is mine, saith the Lord. Just enjoy the day, Jamie.'

As though a snake had slithered out through the rocks of the cairn, Jamie is on his feet on behalf of the old secular Alex. 'What's this religious crap? Christ, you've not turned to religion for comfort?'

He's pleased to have suggested that Alex might be the one in need of comfort even though it was he who initiated the break-up, but this satisfaction melts away before the implication in Alex's last words that they are just enjoying a day together, no more.

'It was only a phrase. I only meant that you can't take on everything. Perhaps I pushed too hard to drag you into my concerns, onto committees and things. You getting mugged stuffing those Iraq leaflets through doors in Possilpark.' He's gathering up both lots of sandwich wrappings.

'So you have that much influence over me, getting me doing things against my will.' ·

'Jamie, you've suffered enough, you can't take on all the world's suffering.'

'Jesus did. I can do Biblical allusions, too. Anyway, I'm not taking on all the world's suffering. Just the dogs' suffering.' And then, to have a pee, he pointedly turns away from the man he slept naked with for two decades, saying as he pees, 'If you had responsibilities only because God handed them out, like an office manager giving out tasks, a celestial e-mail to my desk every day telling me exactly what I've to do … well, then, if I'm not sent the e-mail *Stop the dogs' suffering*, okay, then it's not my responsibility. Not in my job description. But God doesn't exist, so responsibilities aren't limited. It *is* my responsibility. Yours too. Child abuse next door – is that not my business, either? For fuck's sake, just accept that I do distress at cruelty to dogs, you have your standing orders to the Red Cross Disaster Fund and Amnesty.' His anger can't jeopardise getting back together, because what's for you won't go by you. A heat haze dims the higher peaks of Ben Vorlich and Stuc a' Chroin. They're not just more hills: you have to be unimaginably different to be up there.

'I've had to cut back on the standing orders since it's been just my salary, Jamie.'

What does that mean? Still turned away peeing, Jamie can't see Alex's face. Is he supposed to reply, 'Well, it needn't be just *your* salary'? Would they be getting back together, not because Alex still loves you after all and can't believe the awful mistake he made, but because it would facilitate his charitable giving?

And Alex addressing him as 'Jamie' even when there's no-one else around he needs distinguishing from … This habit, thoroughly analysed, discloses a hundred reasons why their relationship was never meant to be. The flood of gratitude Jamie feels for this revelation sends him striding ahead in the descent. A lanky gawky moody teenager of forty-eight stumping off to his room after a family row? So what?

And then he halts: there's movement lower down. A quad bike approaches effortlessly, almost bouncing uphill. This must be the farmer, a laconic and suspicious countryman, zooming up to reprimand them for trespassing even though everyone says there's no law of trespass in Scotland. The quad bike stops a few yards away, releasing silence.

'Nice day,' says the man. Jamie sifts the remark for menace. The long sideburns on the thin age-indeterminate face confirm the man's cruelty to dogs.

'Isn't it?' Alex, cheerily.

The man surveys the view. He's slight like a jockey: could he pull sheep and tractors out of ditches? His denims are too clean. Jamie, who knows about cheap aftershaves, is amazed by a whiff of *Lynx*.

'Have you, like, lost some sheep?' Jamie manages, opening a route to talking about sheepdogs and thence to their suffering. He feels the *Shut up* nudge Alex will give him when he does mention it.

'Not so far as I know,' says the man. It's a well-known technique of intimidation, to postpone what you really have to say. 'Sometimes I just have to get up here. You'll know what I mean. On the hills you can't help feeling grateful you're alive.'

'Grateful to whom or what, exactly?' If Jamie can mount the secularist's challenge on that, why can't he challenge the man about the dogs?

'We liked the carved fence-post at the top.' Alex, affably.

'And up here I'm away from the wife, too.' The man's over-long laugh plainly invites them to join in a jokey moan about demanding wives, and this is plainly oppressive of gays, but protesting about that would be a diversion from going on the attack about the dogs, and then a gobsmack doubles Jamie's confusion when Alex says, 'Well, we're a gay couple but we have our version of the sentiment.'

'No we're not!' Jamie is laughing with astonishment, nothing else.

The man nods. 'You're meant for each other, meant to be.'

But already he's started the quad bike and without so much as a goodbye is skimming up the hill again. His last words could be just sarcastic or contemptuous, yet they resound with a guarantee, recalling tales in which words have mysterious authority because the speaker may seem ordinary, a beggar or a boatman, but is really some legendary supernatural being in disguise, like the Wandering Jew or Jesus or a fey prophesying creature from Gaelic mythology.

Jamie calls after the farmer, '*Meant* for each other? No-one is meant for anyone, because there's no divine wedding planner, no celestial Hello Dolly Levi planning who's to get together with whom.' Now he's ready for Alex and snaps, 'What did you say that for? I mean, you were always so don't-ask-don't-tell-none-of-their-business.'

'Yes, but you always wanted to be more in-your-face about it.'

'Yes, but to lie.'

Will Alex say, 'Well, we could make it true'? But now words must be set aside because here are steep outcrops of rock and you're concentrating on your footing, sometimes gripping the coarse straggly branches of the securely rooted heather. The conversational bleatings of the sheep below and the fields that are an image of peace and blessing produce a homecoming feeling, but once they reach the track leading off the open hillside, the feeling is destroyed by the massed demonic barking from the dog-shed that's reaching new heights of intensity and rage. Mere howling would have produced softer feelings, mere melancholy; this is chaos declaring war.

'Still jumping up-down, up-down in that mad robotic way,' Jamie shouts as he scurries past the open shed. Safely beyond, he adds, 'I'd be as bad as the farmer himself if I stood by and did nothing about it.'

'That's silly, Jamie. These dogs would still have been suffering even if you'd not been here at all. You're not to blame. Your presence or absence makes no difference.'

Alex walks on so slowly that he might have been trying deliberately to avoid an air of having delivered a decisive retort.

And that's when Jamie's eye is caught by the single strand of barbed wire strung above the charming dry-stane dyke that borders the track; caught by a series of black blobs with tiny appendages, each blob hand-stuck on its barb a meticulous four barbs from the next. Beyond the wall a gang of exploring lambs charges about among munching ewes. The blobs are moles, shovel hands and delicate snouts exposed. Jamie begins to count them: an even number and there'll be reunion by nightfall. A blob moves. That has to be the sweet warm gentle spring breeze, no-one could have impaled a live mole.

Suddenly the benign grin in the fence-post dissolves, is gone entirely. There's only dead wood with hacked indentations, the lovely landscape of peace and blessing is a flimsy delusive film projected upon unyielding rock, and the suffering of dogs is nothing but a motion of atoms. Not only is there no-one to hand out duties like an office manager distributing tasks, but the world is not, after all, a limitless domain for the free exercise of conscience, for it's suddenly clear that nothing *matters*.

Jamie hurries to catch Alex up. 'You're right, it's not my business.' It will strike him in the middle of the night, in the midst of happiness, that he left the live twisting mole stuck on its barb, and will reproach himself for fleeing into forgetfulness from the task of horrible mercy-killing.

When Alex drops him at his flat, Jamie asks, 'Do you want to come in?' It's as awkward as an invitation 'for coffee' after a disco decades before.

'I can see where you've been living,' says Alex. More hopeful than *I can see where you live.*

There's mail. Jamie stoops to lift it, Alex shuts the front door behind them as though it were his business to do so.

Leaflet ... phone bill ... postcard from someone Jamie saw a few times last autumn ... another leaflet, about home-delivered pizza.

He turns back to the first leaflet.

'Christ!'

There has to be a reason why this leaflet is here just at this moment. It's from an animal welfare charity. The front shows a starving mongrel with sticking-out ribs and a hurt mournful face that yearns to love you in spite of all the bad you've done. The dog was left in a locked flat when its owner went to America. It pawed a cupboard door ajar and tried to bite open unyielding tins.

'A sign, a message!' Jamie says it ironically, of course. Equally ironically he adds, 'Being sent a message makes you feel sort of noticed. Cherished, even, which I haven't felt much lately.'

'So you got the message! I tried to get it across to you every ten minutes on that bloody hill and thought I'd failed. It's what the man said, Jamie, we are meant to be together. You can't love someone without believing that.' He kisses Jamie.

'No, no,' Jamie says when he can speak again, meaning that Alex misunderstood what message he was referring to, the universe nudging you with a leaflet, an imaginary message, for there aren't any signs or message like that. But Alex will misunderstand that *No, No*, and Jamie quickly covers with, 'You *can* love someone without believing it's meant to be. I do.' It strikes him that the animal welfare people waited to photograph the dog before feeding it.

They say all that is necessary for reunion, then Jamie waves the pizza leaflet and says, 'We've had a sign what the celebration meal's to be. Let's send out for a pizza. Oh, I forgot, you don't eat junk food.'

'I may not have done in the past.'

Jamie picks up the phone and dials, feeling like a character in a book whose author always planned that his time of trial was to have a happy ending. 'I want to report cruelty to dogs on a farm.' He eyes Alex defiantly.

Ron Butlin

THE PHILOSOPHER'S APPRENTICE
(Excerpt from a novel-in-progress)

It was four a.m. when they left Midsummer Madness. Outside the derelict church they stumbled around in the early light, picking their way across the muddy wasteland, careful of half-submerged bricks and timbers, smashed glass, the heaped and abandoned scaffolding, shattered slates. When they came to a gap in the protective hoarding that enclosed the demolition site, the opportunity to help the girl step over an oil-slicked pool gave Hume the perfect excuse to take her hand.

No hanging around, not here. Keep moving, he urged, hurrying them both along street after empty street narrow with boarded-up windows and burnt-out top floors. Front gardens were strewn with old cookers, carpets, broken toys. Stripped of its doors and wheels, a car rusted against a tenement wall, resting chassis-high in uncut grass and dandelions. A few yards further on a mattress that had been gutted and left to rot on the pavement needed sidestepped. No birdsong here, only the occasional screech and scuffle of seagulls among lidless bins.

Keep moving, keep moving. Street after bare street until they reached the main road. Hume slowed down, turned to ask her full name.

'DD, like I said.' She was a little out of breath at the pace he had set.

'Is that short for something?'

'Diana the Damned!' She yelled into the silence of the early morning, then ran off laughing in the direction of town, her high heels clacking.

The Council estate now a good half-hour behind them, Hume was getting seriously impressed. With DD leading the way, they had entered a part of Edinburgh where the socio-economic ratings clicked up at every corner. B3, B2, B1. Here sunlight warmed litter-free streets and hedges, its new-day colours soaking into well-groomed lawns, neat flowerbeds and rockeries. There were front porches, garages, conservatories. From the trees and gabled rooftops, early morning birds celebrated another day of peace and plenty.

As he turned into an even wealthier ghetto of high sandstone walls, wrought iron gates, gravel drives, greenery and secluded mansions, Hume reflected on Seneca. Few philosophers had been particularly well-off – but Seneca had at one point been the richest man in Ancient Rome, only just in time having the good sense to hand over his grandest palace to emperor-pupil Nero, whose jealousy was beginning to look murderous. The search for wisdom and the pursuit of wealth, could they never—?

'Nearly there!' DD called out.

So far, Hume too had scorned luxury with its trappings of arrogance and privilege. But now, surrounded by the kind of affluence and solid success that can only be expressed in upmarket property, he couldn't keep a certain awe out of his voice as he asked:

'You live around *here*?'

'Oh, yes.'

'Really?'

She turned to him. 'Do I look as if I don't?'

'No, no ... Not at all.' Back-pedalling the tone of surprise, he switched to mock-charm: 'For such grace and beauty as yours, anything less than a turreted, three-storey Victorian townhouse would be ...'

She'd come to a stop outside a varnished wooden door set in the sandstone wall that ran along the pavement. She unlocked it.

'You can come in, if you want.'

A moment later, they were standing on a stone-paved path. Two lines of trees arched above them – a guard of honour all but blotting out the early morning light.

The gate was relocked. Then DD was beside him again.

'It's only a small place really,' she said.

'Oh.' Hume nodded.

Only a small place was precisely how Seneca was reputed to have described his dangerously magnificent palace. The rich love to play these games of self-deprecation; making their wealth seem of little consequence, glorifies it even more. Hoping to stay alive a little longer, the wealthy philosopher had, of course, been desperate to be taken at his word.

Further down the path, the trees gave way to a parkland of lawn, bushes, more trees, flowerbeds, trellised greenery against the distant wall. They passed under a second archway to lawn number two – houses like this didn't have *drying-greens*. More flowers, a wooden arbour, more bushes, more trees, a pool where a life-sized stone nymph was bathing. A dozen or so golden brown fish swam around her base.

'They're koi.'

Hume began working on the punchline of a possible joke about how they wouldn't look quite so coy if ... when DD added:

'Worth nearly a hundred pound apiece, some of them.'

No joke then.

'My rent is to feed them twice a day.'

From the back, the townhouse looked even more impressive: full-length windows, ornamental stonework, some stained glass, a couple of balconies. The roof had a shooting-gallery of stone urns set along the edge, a gargoyle at each corner, more chimneys than he'd ever seen on one roof before.

The small wooden summerhouse was painted yellow, with one door, one window, slatted shutters and a smokestack coming out of its green-felted roof. A Marie Antoinette-style imitation shepherd's bothy? It really *was* small.

'Is this where you live?'

'For the moment. Usually I just play here.' She went up the two wooden steps to the door.

Play? Marie Antoinette and her rustic fantasies was maybe not such a bad guess – was it some kind of full-sized dolls' house for adults and their adult games? Sounded promising. He followed her in.

The summerhouse contained an armchair, a bed-settee, a small table, a few shelves. A wood-burning stove stood in the corner. Most of the floor space was taken up by a piano, a baby-grand.

'It's Mrs Chisholm's piano. She lives in the main house. Dora's elderly and doesn't play much now though we sometimes go through some duets. This was her practice room.'

Hume crossed over to the window. The trees, the archways of flowers, the lawns. The nymph was carrying an earthenware pot on her shoulders, tilting as if about to pour herself a shower. There'd probably be a timer-switch to set the water splashing and bubbling over the mossy green nakedness of her stone breasts, hips and legs, to refresh the koi carp swimming below. First light had almost finished colouring in the whole garden. The birds were in full chorus …

Time to move into romantic mode.

Perfect setting. Perfect morning for the perfect summer's day to come. Midsummer Day …

Romantic mode?

Him? Like the usual thrust-and-fuck with his flatmate Cat a few days ago? Settling on master and slave, he'd ordered her to lie on her back, lift up her skirt. As he'd taken her, she'd staged a slaves' revolt, spitting in his face and hissing that he was a shit, a bastard and that she despised him, hated him. Then, as he'd thrust harder, she'd dug her fingers into his back, clung to him, and begged him to fuck her as hard as he could. Good fun at the time but, as always, there'd been the aftertaste of disgust. Not that it had lasted, of course. It never did. Soon enough, the two of them had been at it again. Lust-and-disgust, lust-and-disgust repeated over and over. Like a bad dream. Cat's bad dream? His own?

So far the entire night with DD had been like a dream, too. One of the best ever.

But how soon before Hume's taken her in his arms and kissed her, eased her down onto the bed? For then a very different dream would take over, a familiar dream that would follow its usual route to its predictable end. That done, he'd wake up. Abruptly. Wondering how to make his excuses and leave.

He turned away from the window, ready to take DD in his arms.

As a little girl DD had learned to slow down her heartbeat at will. With practice, and if she concentrated hard enough, she could sometimes arrest it completely. Standing legs apart, feet pressed down onto the floor, she'd hold her breath, tensing every muscle until her whole body locked rigid, her fists clenched so tight her fingernails cut into the palms of her hands ... When it seemed she could bear it no longer, she'd let go all at once, and her heart would start beating again. It felt like a dam bursting. Utterly, utterly glorious. She'd cry out with relief, jump into the air, run round and round in circles like a dog crazy at the sheer exuberance of it all. The ecstasy of coming alive once more.

Her first 'coming alive' as she began to call it, happened when she was four. She'd been about to leave her room to rush downstairs and out of the house to play in the sunshine. But she didn't. She couldn't. Instead, she found herself rooted to the spot and repeating into herself, *I won't go, I won't go.*

Quite unable to move, and with her heart slowing down ...

She wanted to be outside playing in the sun, she really longed to be there ...

The flower pattern on her wall, her pink bedspread, the picture of white horses running along a beach – everything around her now seemed so very *intense*, charged with an almost unbearable sense of anticipation. Glorious, and yet terrifying—

Finally her heartbeat stopped completely. That moment of terrifying stillness – the certain knowledge that from then on she would live as if held on the palm of someone's hand, a hand that might close around her at any moment and crush her.

With a sudden rush, she came alive for the first time. A year or so later when she heard about hell, she immediately recognised it – for she *knew* terror already. That was when she secretly re-christened herself, adapting the nickname her parents had given her and which stood for Darling Daughter and Darling Diana, to her own version – Diana the Damned. For DD, hell remained close ever since.

This new man she'd met for the first time only a few hours earlier? Standing at the window with his back to her. Shy? Screwing up his courage?
  She went across to him.

After they had made love, new man Hume asked her to play something on the piano.
  'Nothing too romantic and dreamy,' he said. 'Something with real soul.'
  'Mozart?'
  'Always sounds like eighteenth-century muzak. Too many wigs and buckles.'
  'Oh?' So much for the greatest composer ever. 'How about this, then?' A Chopin *nocturne*, with maximum expression and feeling. Things didn't come any better.
  As she played, Chopin provided the soundtrack to her edited review of the night's highlights. That disco in the abandoned church, meeting this new man, walking home together through the deserted streets … Hume was all charm – *surface* charm. What lay beneath would be far more interesting, it had to be. Like most men, of course, he couldn't see beyond his own cleverness, his own glibness, and had succeeded in totally charming himself. It would be hard work to dig beneath, gouging down to get to what really mattered. Plenty of time though. Until last night she'd never told anyone her secret name. So why had she told *him*, Mr Glib, of all people? Why had she shouted it at him before running off down the street? If he runs after me, she'd bargained with herself, I'll let him sleep with me. So she had.
  She shrugged, then glanced across to the bed to see how His Glibness was taking Chopin.
  With his eyes closed, it seemed.
  Cloth-eared bastard.
  She was about to wake him up with some jagged Bartok when that familiar part-ecstatic, part-terrifying sense of dread suddenly swept over her. She caught her breath.

The spread of black and white keys lying under her hands, the polished wood of the piano, the stool she sat on, the new man lying nearby on the bed, early morning flooding over his face as though he might be drowned in sunlight …

By the time her heartbeat and breathing had returned to normal, all that remained were the nail marks on her palms, like faint stigmata.

Martin Connor

PRIMARY

I burned at being
   unable to breathe the song
and swell back into that dead house sparrow
found on the close green

so I turned away
   from the fence of the world's
words, to look for the stile of my breaking
free and making red.

I learned that no wish
   could let that sparrow up
to once again try on its tiny back
the colossal blue

and for years now
   I've yearned for the hidden life
that animates the green and red and blue
to let me in and know.

George Craig

SPINNING

There's a window above the shops in Hyndland, just where the road Ts and traffic splits straight ahead or downhill. I noticed it last month, the day after I'd seen John Edward. I lifted my head and there it was. I thought it was someone's birthday, cards stuck to the glass – the way mums tie balloons to railings to show other parents where little so-and-so's party is. But I passed it again the following week and realised I'd been wrong. It was postcards on the windows, foreign cards, lots of them. Cuts of cardboard stuck onto the bubbled glass with little blobs of blue at their corners.

I've walked up that hill, once a week, every week for twenty-odd years, carrying home my butcher-meat, individual portions of flesh wrapped in thin white plastic inside my canvas shopping bag. I'd never raised my eyes from street-level until then. But now it's the first thing I notice. And I love it. I hurry through Tuesday chores to get to the shops, humph my bag full of messages up the hill, hit the brow and take in all the views in that huge bay, its middle window scattered with sandy beaches, national flags and monuments, olive-skinned girls dressed in pelts of flowers, surfer-dudes riding boards. And almost every week, there's a new picture up of life outside the window, beyond that street.

But it always makes me think, why am *I* the one looking at the good side? If that was my window, I'd turn those rectangles around, let the sun halo them, let the pictures light up *my* interior. And I'd never pull the curtains at night. I'd let evening streetlamps frame an orange glow around the idea of those places.

I have theories. Maybe this person gets cards from a lover away on a long journey and prefers to see the loops of their words dance inside the room. Or maybe they're from scattered family members, sending fragments to hold their loved-one together until they're reunited. But, in the end, I return to the same conclusion, that this is just someone trying to communicate, showing the best of what they have. Turning the good side out to the street and hiding behind that façade, trying to connect even if the thought terrifies them.

I know because it's the same for me. People have looked at me funny ever since I was a wee boy. I've lived here all my life and still they look at me kind of peculiar. It doesn't matter what I do, or how I dress it, they try to look past the picture I present them with, try to see what's behind my M&S smart-casuals, my wet-look gel, my Paco Rabanne. Twenty-three years is a long time but when they look at me that way I know that they remember the headlines—

WEST END PRAYS FOR CYCLE-CRASH BOY
LOCAL YOUTH SUFFERS BIKE ACCIDENT BRAIN DAMAGE

—and they look at me funny because they know it wasn't the way the papers told it. There were witnesses, lots of them: sales assistants, lady lunchers and afternoon shoppers, the way I am now on my day out. That was a Tuesday as well. And it was bright. But everything was brighter then. I remember there was more colour in curtains, more sparkle, and the sun made rainbows of them. And that was what folk told the reporters, as I sat on the kerb, covered in witness-coats, being brought teeny wee glasses of juice as we waited for the ambulance:

—*Oh yes, ah saw the whole thing. The boy had no chance wi' that bloody sun in his eyes.*

—*I've been writing to the Council for years to get lights at that junction. It's a death trap.*

—*Poor sowel mustabeen blindet cyclin doon that hill on his wee bike wi aw they mirrors oanit.*

And that was what they wrote. And people comforted me, because people were kinder then, not always looking for someone to blame like they do now. They wanted to think that you were kind too, preferred to think of life as accidental rather than malicious. The newspapers put it down to the handlebars, down to the cycle design. Said that Raleigh Choppers should be banned because they put your hands into your line of vision. Said it was a blessing, me being the first in the street to wear a helmet and started a petition to change things. Then the man from the sports company visited Mum and Dad and drank stewed tea out of Gran's china and said we could make big money if they told how my helmet had saved me and took my photo and said that these things happen and it shouldn't be allowed to ruin two lives.

But they didn't ask me. Not once. Not the police, or the nurses, or the journalists, or the company man or Mum and Dad. So I didn't say. I took my exams while John Edward lay in hospital with a burst head. I got into Tech while he went back to school, back two years, into remedial. I got a career, while he scraped into a jannie's job at the same school he'd never left. And I never told a single soul.

So I tried to forget about it and get on with things, as you do. But it creeps up on you, then it's always there, even when you think it's not or that it doesn't matter any more because it was ages ago and who remembers anyway? Because it does matter and they do remember and eventually they look at you funny. And it's still there, all the time, it eats into you and swells and festers.

Then the late work starts, then the lost clients, the three-day weeks and the doctor's incapacity line and the relief when Mum goes and Dad follows and you're left with the flat so you don't have to go outside any more – except on Tuesdays for the shopping, because you have to and on Thursday nights, on European nights, to watch the football on the big screen at the hotel, because the therapist thinks it's good to get out and socialise (even if you do sit at the back of the bar where you can't see the screen for the pillar and no-one else sits there because of it).

And still I don't tell, I don't talk about it – even in the bar, even on the couch. But I keep going back there to that junction every week, marking the spot. I get my butcher-meat and humph my canvas shopping bag up the hill to where it happened. Until I found the window, I always used to stop there at that point in the street and look down and feel it all over again, relive the before and after. Re-run the *fuckyou Johnny-boy if you can't move your arse fast enough to cross the bloody road, cos there's no stoppin me now pal, cos I'm on my Raleigh Chopper, 5-speed, Mark 2, T-bar gearshift and better than a BMX any bloody day pal, so get your feet runnin, cos I'm pedlin fast as fuck – tot'ly invincabul!*

Then that same feeling again: the all-over cold sweat; the slow screech; the head-over-heels; the melon-splatter of that poor bastard's head seeping all over the road, all over my clothes and my bike's twisted frame, with the front wheel that won't stop spinning. And afterwards knowing *I've done bad and I have to tell when I do bad* - but no-one asking, avoiding the question – and knowing *I've got to hide it, they want me to hide it.* And after a while telling myself, *no-one wants to know anyway, and I was only thirteen anyway, and you can't live your life with regrets anyway.* But knowing the whole time that they're looking at me funny and that maybe they always will now.

I saw him last month – John Edward – *Johnny-boy.* I'd heard about him over the years and I'd visited him once after the accident, when he was still in hospital, but he didn't see me, not really. And he didn't see me again, at the hotel, last month.

It was a Thursday night. One of the London clubs was playing a foreign team in green. The woman arrived first. I watched her through the French doors that separate the back of the bar from the restaurant. Once the crowd get into the game, I usually pull back the voile curtains and look through at the people eating courses, being all social with each other, and wonder what secrets they're hiding between mouthfuls.

The woman ordered a drink and fidgeted with the end of the tablecloth, twisting it into a crimp. She looked at the restaurant entrance every few seconds. Then he walked in, suit hanging off him and a kind of a heavy brow pushing down on his face – tall and lean and could have been handsome, except he looked like he couldn't get enough air in. He approached her and shook her hand, the way you do the first time you meet a stranger. She wore a wedding band on the wrong hand, but he had none.

I shared their date, watched them avoid eye contact, mistime their jokes, almost manage to touch hands. I was rooting for him, cheering in his direction from the back of the bar every time one of the telly teams scored. But, after the meal, they sat through too many coffees, not quite smiling, then she dabbed a kiss on his cheek and left. And I thought, well at least he's trying – you're still alive in there, Johnny-boy. Then he turned and looked at me through the French door-glass, stared me out, and then nothing. He up and paid his way and left and didn't look back at my face.

It was the following Tuesday that I first noticed the window with the postcards above the shops. And now it gives me something else to look at, something new to think about when I'm there. Now, I climb that hill with my week's butcher-meat and I don't have to look down for the stains on the street. And I don't feel so alone any more, because the sunlight hits the postcards and gives me a friend on the other side of that window, someone else who puts a face on things, so people don't see behind. Because folk nowadays don't make excuses, they wouldn't tolerate it, they like revenge. But I don't think that's what he wants.

Seth Crook

MAGRITTE MACPHAIL

*It is a union that suggests the essential mystery of the world. Art for me is not an
end in itself, but a means of evoking that mystery.*

René Magritte, on putting seemingly unrelated objects
together in juxtaposition.

A rusting this,
a dented, pot shaped that,
an oatgrinder, half a caravan

the other half
slumped, sinking in the field,
sprouting a telly,
a welly

all evoking
the essential mystery
of the world
(west highland office)

and scattering it
across the croft,
like the rusted parts
of an old Trabant.

But, lone piper
of the unexplained,
do we need surrealism
and its strange signs?

We have the fairy mounds,
the circles,
fluctuating broadband.

Anna Crowe

CUTTING MY FATHER'S HAIR

This morning, the birds' water-bowl
was frozen, coarse frost trapping
a few ragged scraps of down.
When I prised off the thick lid,
the underside was a bed of moss-
crystals, winter's ephemera;
a brash of ice-fronds, a fern-
forest astonishing in its beauty;
each fragile stem spatulate,
growing a lobe

as delicately rounded
as this that I must fold back
out of the way of my scissors.
Grey wisps of hair drift down
like the feathers of strange birds.
The rims of your ears
are frosty with eczema.
Towel around your shoulders
you sit, remote in your deafness;
shrouded like heavy furniture
in a cold, empty house.

Ever Dundas

WIRE

Worm

The Prime Minister clawed his way out of the mouth. There was a violence to it that made me nauseous. I read on, as I always did, staring into the camera lens, affecting composure.

'Inex 2020s will soon become obsolete. The Endostream 2025 is currently being tested and will be ready to launch in a few months. David Kincaid, the spokesperson for ...'

When the Prime Minister freed himself from the mouth he slithered on the ground like a worm, enveloped in viscous fluid.

'... demonstrating the Endo 25, he showed that it would lie just beneath the skin of the arm, where a small control panel can be accessed.'

The meaning of the words were lost. They disappeared into the mouth, they shimmered across the body of the Prime Minister and sank into the fluid as he squirmed.

'... with a single thought the subject can access all online content, open up their messaging service, and connect to other subjects.'

I paused. The words were regurgitated by the gaping mouth. I felt myself slipping in, but pulled back.

'There is the continual stream of recorded data that can be accessed at any time, just as it can be with the Inex 2020, but without the need of an external intermediary. What do you think? Are you ready to give up your Inex? What impact will this have on a global scale? Will this further divide the rich and poor? Contact us, and tell us your thoughts. Here's Karen with the weather.'

I was proud of my finely honed charm, sure of myself. The screen went blank before reflecting the bright lights of the studio. I flinched, unable to tolerate the lights. I rummaged for my pills, but the box was empty. I scrunched my eyes closed. A door slammed, and I heard my name.

Black Hole

I watched her approach, moving in and out of focus like a shimmering mirage, burned by the lights. My body ached. I needed protection. I needed to be numb.

'What the hell was that?'

Her face was just a black hole with a halo of piercing light.

'What was what?'

'You damn well know what. You lose it on air one more time and you're up for review. Where's your Inex?'

'At home.'

'No one goes out without their Inex. No one. Shit, get Ken on now. We can't have this idiot screwing up the next segment. Go home. Go home and sort yourself out.'

The black hole disappeared and I fumbled for my shades.

Desiring Machine

The floor was a mass of writing bodies. Candyfloss oozed from their eyes and between their legs. It crawled up the cameras, over the newsdesk. I was enveloped by the pungent sweetness, pulled in by tentacle-limbs, and sugar-coated lips. I sucked a penis tumescent with candyfloss, gorging until I was sick. They devoured my vomit. Sticky clouds wrapped around my ankles as I crawled to the exit.

'Go home,' she called to me, 'and get some rest.'

There was no candyfloss, just an expression of pity. I opened the door.

Fixed Assemblage

Caram was leaning against the wall, a cigarette dangling from his lips. The Inex perched on his shoulder, its spidery limbs reaching round his neck. Like every Inex, it unnerved me. Most people cultivated the childlike appearance, exaggerating their cuteness with colourful clothes and bows, but Caram's was always naked. Its blank eyes met my gaze, and I looked away, feeling the nausea double. I stared at Caram. His eyes were closed, face turned towards the sun. His black hair was swept back, strands stroking his jawline. Caram's body flowed as liquid, an ichorous seduction.

'What are you doing here?'

'I thought you might need something.'

I made my way towards him, stilted, my body turned in on itself.

'The touching concern of a drug dealer.'

Caram shrugged, looking away.

'Let's go to the bar. I'll fix you up.'

I nodded. He reached out, as if to take me by the arm, before pushing his hands into his pockets, hunching his shoulders. He mirrored me; turned in, head bowed, as if the thought of touching me had infected him.

'I can't feel like this anymore,' I said.

'What do you feel?'

'Everything.'

'I'll fix you up,' he said.

The Hallway

Caram walked ahead of me, as if we weren't together. The city passed by in a blur of people. I kept to the inside of the pavement, my fingers sliding across shop windows. I stopped at one of the stores. The mannequins walked along the length of the window display. One of them turned and stopped in front of me, pausing to give me time to look at the clothes, before it turned away and was replaced by another. The mannequins were blank, erased. A shift in focus, and I could see my reflection overlaid on a mannequin's absent face. I removed my shades. I shifted slightly, contemplating my image falling off the side of the mannequin. It looked grotesque. My features corrupted the simplicity. I crouched, sliding down the glass. My eye flashed silver, cut through by the glint of sequins on the mannequin's dress. I stared at my hand pressed against the glass. My skin was translucent. My nails were ragged. I pulled one of them free and found metal underneath.

'We're here,' Caram said.

I looked up.

'We're here. Just around the corner.'

I left the window, watching the mannequin turn and walk away.

The Eternal Recurrence

I was safe, closed off. I pulled away my nails. I didn't feel anything. The metal underneath was smooth, perfect. He joined me, sitting opposite, placing a bottle of vodka and two glasses on the table next to his Inex. It looked like a discarded doll. Its eyes glowed.

'I need something,' I said, drumming my fingers against the glass, the metal clicking.

He lifted the bottle and raised his eyebrows. I watched him pouring it and shook my head.

'Something else, something more.'

'Well, that's what we're here for, isn't it? How did those pills do you?'

My news channel was on the screen behind the bar. Ken's face was huge.

'I don't know,' I said, turning away from the screen. 'I think they messed with my head.'

'They're supposed to mess with your head. Isn't that what you're after?'

'Not like this.'

'You hallucinating?'

I nodded, knocking back my drink.

'You just need a different strength. I've got what you need right here.'

'Yeah?'

'Sure. Cigarette?'
'Stop messing with me.'
'I'm not. Be patient. What's the rush?'
Caram's Inex poured me more vodka.
'Where's your Inex?'
'At home.'
'Don't you miss it?'
'Some people say they love their Inex and really mean it. It's their best friend.'
'You don't feel that way?'
'It's just wires and synthetic flesh.'
I knocked back the vodka.

Black Haze

'Legislation banning the rearing of animals for meat has been passed amidst controversy that has unexpectedly united the pro-meat lobby and animal rights activists against environmentalists. Synthetic meat has been cheaply mass-produced in a bid to curb the environmental impact of rearing animals. In concert with radical changes in family planning, synthetic meat production has contributed hugely to the reduction in famines and the recovery of several developing countries after years of poverty. The animal rights lobby criticise the legislation for not implementing a plan of action for animal welfare. Some groups have barricaded themselves in farms, and the mass-slaughter of animals has sparked riots.'

I pressed my hands against my ears.

'Sometimes,' I said, 'You don't want to be plugged in.'

'Disconnect,' said Caram.

The booth had been closed off for smoking, but now we were fully private. Enclosed with Caram in this darkness, the worry faded. My fingers click-clacked against the table and I drank the vodka. I sat, hunched, staring at him, comforted by him, disappearing into his beauty and the beginnings of a vodka haze.

Caram lit up and sucked on the cigarette, smoke coiling out of his lips. I breathed it in. I watched his lips curl around it, the moisture he left. He offered it to me, and I took it, staring at the glistening shape his lips left behind. I licked it.

He lit one for himself and settled into the booth, leaning back, spreading his arms out across the back of the seat. I was jealous of his ease, folded in on myself, waiting for the drink to really kick in. He was opened up to me, exposed as I sat scrunched up. I licked it again. He smiled, and I placed it in my mouth. We contemplated each other from across the divide of the table, sucking on cigarettes, knocking back vodka. Silence.

Better Than Any Drug

I stared at the cuts and burns weaving their way down Caram's arms. Some were a silver-white that sparkled in a shaft of light, others were the dense black-red of still-healing scabs. I wanted to pick at the scabs, opening up the old wounds to feel inside him.

I took a long draw on my cigarette, burning it right down, feeling the heat on my lips, hearing it crackle. I stubbed it out in the ashtray and watched as wires emerged from my arm. They slithered, coiling around my wrist and entering my skin again, disappearing at the base of my hand. I looked away, taking another drink.

He leant on the table, nursing his vodka, stroking the lighter. I took another cigarette, sliding the lighter from between his fingers. The wires in my hand quivered. I ignored them, lighting up.

Eat Me, Drink Me

'So what do you have for me?'

Caram took a drag on his cigarette as he reached into his pocket and placed a silver box on the table.

'That's all you need in there.'

I flicked it open. Six red pills.

'They won't mess with my head?'

He leaned in.

'You'll float.'

He waved his hand through the cigarette smoke.

'Alright.'

I pulled out some cash and placed it on the table. Dropping my cigarette into the ashtray, I popped one of the pills, washing it down with vodka. He lifted my cigarette, leant back and licked it. The tightness in my body eased. I felt myself unfurl.

Wired

Caram watched me, my cigarette now clamped between his lips.

'And we float,' he said.

I nodded. He smiled.

I stared at my metal nails, the vibrating wires. They didn't concern me. I possessed his ease.

He flicked cigarette ash into the ashtray and I leaned forward, stroking the scars on his arm.

'What does it feel like?' I asked.

'Better than nothing,' he said.

'I've always wanted to feel nothing.'

'It's not what it's cracked up to be.'

I took his cigarette and stubbed it out on the back of my hand.

'I can't feel it.'

'It's the drugs. There's no point in doing it if you don't need to.'

'I want to know what it's like to be you.'

'It doesn't feel like anything.'

I pushed my finger into the burn. Nothing. I dragged away the damaged skin and found metal underneath.

'I'm hallucinating.'

'What do you see?'

'Metal. Wire.'

'I'll go home with you.'

'Home?'

'I'll look after you. Until the hallucinations pass.'

'I'm not frightened. I feel good now.'

'You need me.'

'I don't need you. I want to be you.'

He shook his head.

'Just let the pill kick in.'

'I'm becoming machine.'

'I'll take you home.'

Revol

Caram sought out my hidden hands.

'Can you feel the metal? Can you feel the wire?'

Caram nodded, leaning in. Closing his eyes, he slid his hand across my neck, feeling the wires weaving in and out of my skin. He pressed in closer, pulling my head back. He slid his tongue across my lips. My fingers were entwined in his hair, the wires in my wrist weaving across his head, feeling their way over his skin, pulling him closer. We kissed and my tongue cut through his. The wires slid across his neck, and I could feel his pulse increase as blood and oil filled our mouths, spilling down our throats, over our lips. The wires snaked over his shoulder, encircling his arm, entering the still-healing wounds. He watched the wires disappear. I was inside him, tasting beneath his skin. His head fell back, his mouth open, blood-oil glistening on his lips.

He threaded his fingers through my hair.

Broken

'How are the hallucinations?'

The wires slithered across the furniture.

'I'm becoming furniture.'

Caram smiled, shook his head.

'I'll get you a drink.'

I was hot, nauseous. Sweat glistened on my body like black oil. My skin broke open, oil-sweat oozed from the wounds. Wires emerged all over me. I called to Caram, only to spew out blood-oil. My body was burning. I stared at my reflection in the mirror. My silver eyes shed rivulets of oil. I watched as the skin on my lips broke apart, disappearing into the black oil that dribbled from my mouth. I reached to touch my face, the tendons in my arm snapping, skin and muscle falling away.

Drink Me, Eat Me

I felt like I was on fire.

'I have your drink.'

'I'm burning.'

I crawled into the bath, the cold water enveloping me.

'Can you hear me?'

'I'm becoming water.'

'What are you doing?'

I floated, shedding my skin and muscle. Oil blackened the water.

'I'm floating.'

'Shit. Let me in.'

Caram hammered on the door.

'You're tripping, you could drown.'

I could hear him throwing himself at the door, but it didn't give way. I lay still, staring at the ceiling. Clumps of skin, muscle, and hair gathered on the surface of the water. Wires crept over the side of the bath, exploring the floor and reaching up to the ceiling.

'I'm still hallucinating,' I said. 'Caram? I need more pills.'

The Origin Myth
'I'm floating,' I said.
   'Shit. What a goddamn mess.'
   I looked up to see a woman in army fatigues.
   'I had everything under control,' said Caram.
   'Get this idiot out of my way.'
   'Yes, ma'am.'
   She leaned over me.
   'How do you feel?'
   'I've become machine.'
   'I know,' she said. 'We're here to help.'
   'The pill didn't work.'
   'Everything will be fine.'
   She stood, gesturing towards the hall.
   'Bring the stretcher.'
   'Yes, ma'am.'
   They gave me a pill and the wires retracted. They carried me through
the hall. I heard her speaking through her Inex.
   '... Mid-recall. A malfunction and guardian incompetence. Yes, I will.
Everything is under control.'
   I saw Caram.
   'Hey,' I said.
   'Hey.'
   'I'm still hallucinating.'
   'I know.'

Waiting for the End of Time
She put a gun to Caram's head. Blood spattered across me as they carried
me to the door.
   'Caram ... The damn pill didn't work. I'm still hallucinating.'
   'He knows,' said the woman. 'It will all be fine.'
   'I want to be him. I can taste his blood. I can still taste him.'
   She shook her head.
   'Just let the pill kick in.'
   'The damn pill won't work.'
   'The pill will work.'
   'I'm becoming machine.'
   'Don't worry,' she said. 'We're taking you home.'

Reception

I watched the make-up artist apply rouge to Kincaid's cheeks as the technology segment was airing. It charted the death of mobiles and the rise of the Inex, ending with a still of a child holding the hand of her Inex, overlaid with the words 'IS THIS THE END OF INEX 20?' Three, two, one, and it cut to the studio.

'David,' I said, 'It's been a few months since we last spoke. Where do things stand with the Endo 25?'

'Endostream 25 will be launched next week at the Global Sustainability Conference. We've been working on this for years, so we're all extremely excited. We can't wait to bring this to the public.'

'David, we've invited calls from viewers, and Ann from East London would like to share her concerns. Ann?'

'I love my Inex,' said Ann. 'I couldn't do without it. I use it to do the household chores.'

'Exactly,' said Kincaid, 'You can have the best of both worlds with the Inex 20 and the Endo 25. You can get on and do the important things, with access to everything you need in your own body. The Inex has already been rolled out by various charitable bodies to assist with manual labour in developing countries, in aid work, and in medicine. And, of course, it is used extensively by the military, who we are working closely with on further advancements so that *your* sons no longer come home in body bags. Many people fear that the Inex will become obsolete. That isn't the case. Their use will simply be transferred, freeing us up to become the best we can be with the Endo 25.'

I turned to the camera. I could see my face reflected in the lens. I was serene. I was perfect.

'Thank you for your calls. We don't have time to hear from everyone, but many of our callers have concerns about the cost of the Endo 25. David, some have said that the price is exclusionary. What would you say to them?'

'It's what the market demands. We've had thousands of pre-orders. If people want it, they'll buy it. The Endo 25 will be a boost to the national economy.'

'Thank you, David. Now, lastly, tell us – what does the future hold?'

'We're all cyborgs now,' he said. 'This is our future.'

David Eyre

A SMALL BIRTH: NEW YEAR

Standing by a wood
in the middle of a wet day
wild
with the great wind of the Big Bang
blowing through me
droplets of time

moments in their millions
moving wavelike
to me, from me,
drenching me as they pass,
leaving me restless,
thirsty,

but I put down
the hood of my coat
and bared my head to them
feeling rain
on my face
the first time of my life.

David Eyre

NOLLAIG BHEAG

Nam sheasamh ri taobh coille
ann am meadhan latha fliuch
fiadhaich
agus gaoth làidir a' Mhòr-Spreadhaidh
a' sèideadh tromham
boinneagan tìm

mòmaidean nam muilleanan
a' gluasad ann an tuinn
thugam agus bhuam
gam dhrùdhadh san dol seachad
gam fhàgail anacrach
pàiteach

ach chuir mi dhìom
abaid mo chòta
agus sheall mi ceann-rùisgte riutha
a' faireachdainn uisge
air m'aodann
a' chiad uair nam bheatha.

Olivia Ferguson

LAIRD GOES EAST

Laird went on a business trip. He woke his wife to say goodbye.

The smell of aloe vera gel rose off Jeanette when she hugged him. She was in the habit of rubbing the gel into her elbows before going to bed; it kept the dark wrinkled skin on her elbows from getting dry and flaky, she said. Morning and night, the master suite smelled like a very expensive hospital.

'I'm going to Egypt.'

'You didn't tell me,' she said.

'I don't make a million per year for staying home.'

'Don't drink too much with Stephen.'

It was routine for Laird, whenever he flew east, to book a layover in Montreal and stay with his son, Stephen, for a day or two.

'Okay, I won't,' said Laird, hovering low over Jeanette. She made a kiss quick at his neck. He wasn't sure if she'd wanted to kiss him there, or if his mouth was an inch too far.

Laird drove north along the Elbow from Bel-Aire, over the Bow River, east to the freeway. Some months had passed since the flood, when hundreds of the people living by the Bow, the Little Bow, the Elbow, the Red Deer River, the Sheep River, and the South Saskatchewan River lost everything they had, but the Calgary Stampede was not cancelled. As Laird crossed the Bow he watched all kinds of dreck creep on by. From time to time you could see something big, like a truck with smashed windows, or a broken dredging anchor.

It cost him over $120 to park in the long-stay zone at the airport. The business trips soon added up: each year, he charged thousands of dollars' worth of parking to the expense account. Most of the trips were to Yemen, but this summer they had a shot at a new contract.

He wanted domestic departures. He scanned the atrium for the familiar bands of red, and the red leaf on white, then looked again for his flight number. He'd cut it fine. They were doing the last boarding call just as he exited security. He hurried down the grey buzz-cut carpet to his gate. The woman waiting glowered at him, and his passport picture glowered back at her.

He was the last person down the tunnel walkway. As he stepped across the gap between the walkway and the waiting plane, he got a whiff of early-morning air: cold bright stuff that set him back to a school day at

quarter past six in the morning. Colgate between his teeth. Sweatshirt
with Cadger's Brig embroidered over one nipple.

Laird never said a word on the bus to school; he hadn't properly woken
up yet. He was tired and hungry, because he didn't like eating his breakfast
in those days, but even so he was fine. He just looked out the window and
enjoyed himself.

Silently Laird sat down to his fifty-four-year-old self in executive class.
He watched Calgary drop away, and drank a Clamato. Kissing, being rich,
having his name on a website: in his school days, all those things had been
in the future. These days, didn't he have everything to remember, and
nothing left to imagine?

Laird knew what he liked, and he had it more or less all the time.
It wasn't bad.

He reclined his seat until he was horizontal, and slept again.

*

Once in Montreal, Laird went straight to Stephen's apartment. He took
the metro instead of a taxi, telling himself he'd buy a good bottle of wine
at the restaurant tonight. The metro station was lined with ads of a woman
selling bottled water, her face, her breasts, her hair half-covered with SALE
PUB SEXISTE stickers.

He'd bought the apartment for his son two years ago. Stephen would
stay there for another year while he finished up his degree. Then Laird
would sell the place, hopefully make money on it. He couldn't stand to
think about anyone in his family paying rent.

Stephen was gay, living with a Quebecois boy called Hubert. Laird
imagined his son at forty. Maybe still having sex with Hubert. He thought
about it. Maybe when Stephen was forty he'd still live in the walk-up,
shovelling snow off the stairs in the winter, drinking beer on patios in the
summer, every day speaking the language he, Laird, couldn't learn if he
tried. He heaved his wheelie suitcase up those treacherous stairs, making
a lot of noise, and Stephen opened the door before he could let himself in.

'Didn't know if you'd be home.'

'I got your email. Made a reservation for tonight, too. Careful on
the stairs.'

Stephen took the suitcase from Laird and carried it up the next flight
of stairs. He had on a lightweight sports jacket, over a white shirt. He had
the start of a beard, which looked like iron filings round his chin. Laird
noticed that there was a bracelet on his wrist, made of wooden beads and
technicolour portraits of saints: a nun holding a burning heart, and what
looked like Jesus Christ in a kilt, next to her. Stephen led him through to

the kitchen. With the red sports jacket and that, he looked like the guys Laird saw at the airport in Sicily. He held him close for a moment. Hubert sat watching them.

'Did you eat? When's your flight?' asked Stephen.

He'd told Stephen that he was going to London for a conference.

'Sunday night. Weird time. You look like a – Catholic footie fan,' said Laird.

'Yeah, a bro from Little Italy,' said Hubert.

That made Stephen laugh. Hubert was speaking English to him because Laird was there. True, he could read French a bit, but in Quebec whole sentences passed him by. When he left the room, Stephen and Hubert started up in French again. They rarely used English for anything but swearing.

Laird put his rucksack on the camp bed Stephen had set up for him in the spare room, and connected to the wi-fi. He had made plans to Skype with his brother today, forgetting that he would be with his son in Montreal. There was a message waiting for him. *8pm my time, 3pm your time works.*

'We're going to return these DVDs,' Stephen called to him. 'Come with us, or stay here? We're going to the park after. It's almost three already.'

'I have to Skype with your uncle. I'll meet you at the restaurant.'

'The reservation's for seven. See you later.'

Laird logged on and waited several minutes before clicking Call, even though he could see that John was online too. He didn't want to appear eager. Caring, but not eager. After all, he was busy. He was very busy.

In the weeks since he last spoke to John, two sandstorms had hit Morayshire, covering the fields with dunes. On John's own farm near Forres, the cash crops had all but disappeared under the sand. John sent Laird photographs as they spoke. When he heard 'dunes,' Laird immediately thought of pyramids, camels moving their tall shadows past immense mountains of sand. John's photos showed him a layer of sand on a flat landscape. No dune was more than four feet tall. It looked like a beach on the east coast of Scotland, except that there was no sea.

'We lost a small percentage,' said John. 'It took a few days to clear the fields. We did it with snow ploughs.'

Laird had told John before about the oil fields in Yemen and Egypt, and the methods of hydrocarbon exploration. Now that he was no longer an engineer, but Director of Operations, he found it harder to tell John about his work. It wasn't that things were harder to explain. There were a lot of silences on John's end. Laird didn't flatter himself that the silences stood for envy, or puzzlement; he knew they stood for boredom. So he spoke as though his life had not changed, and told John not about board meetings and business-class flights, but about the difficulties of the new project, and the oil fields. Sometimes they argued, gently, avoiding what was obviously personal, determined that they would not raise their voices, even at this distance.

'Field's the wrong word,' John would say. 'Fields are for growing.'

Fields are what you put fences around, thought Laird. He knew better than to fight with his brother over the meaning of fields. John had left school at sixteen, to join their dad on the farm. Now there was a shop and a café on the farm, and John was one of the suppliers for a national corporation.

Laird remembered picking strawberries for their dad during the summer holidays. He remembered standing beside John in a field of cattle. He and John clutched long sticks in their hands, stretched their arms out and walked forward, hoping for the cows to turn and run pursued by boy giants. Cows were stupid creatures, Dad said. Hold a stick and they'd think it was part of your arm.

'I thought there was a travel advisory for Egypt right now,' said John.

'Nothing to worry about. The guys we're consulting with, they'll see to that.'

Laird was annoyed when John seemed to accept his explanation immediately. No more questions? No more concern? But then it occurred to him that if John asked real questions, he should answer truthfully that nothing could go wrong. They'd assured him that while he was in Egypt he'd see little more than the inside of the airport, the inside of a taxi, the inside of a hotel, and the inside of a boardroom – all of which would be secured by armed guards. And so he dropped it, and let John talk about the farm.

John told him about the new lambs and the Shire horses.

'What are their names?' Laird asked. 'I hope you didn't name anything after me this year.'

'Oh,' said John, 'the lambs don't have names now that the girls are grown up. And the horses are still called Prince, Clyde, and Glory.'

*

Laird left the apartment at six thirty. The trees were making a right mess of the street with their berries. *But there's no chuggy on the sidewalk,* he noted approvingly, *not like some places.* He kept to one side, steering clear of the businesspeople and students heading to the metro.

The tarmac on the roads was grey and patched with thick black liquorice lines, just like in his hometown. Was there no money to redo the roads?

And yet Montreal was a thriving city, not a dead town of hairdressers and ring-road supermarkets. Last thing he'd heard, the old grammar school building was demolished to build more housing. For decades it had been a commuter town. It made more sense to him to live close to your job, leave the empty kirks and the Whuppity Scoorie to other folk.

Laird turned left, then right, then right again. He wasn't sure of the way to the restaurant now. His phone buzzed. Stephen had sent him a text asking where he was. Seven o'clock came and went. He didn't know where he was going. He began to pass doorways that turned out to be gated alleyways. Some kids, teenagers probably, laughed in that darkness. Not at him, surely. They had smartphones and clinking backpacks. Two white boys and a black girl.

Then he felt and heard a disturbance in the street behind him. Strides toward him, too fast for him to turn around. He saw her somehow, without turning around. She hit Laird hard on both shoulders. She smacked him with the palms of her hands and kept pushing. He heard her breathe and laugh. He fell forward, he fell forward onto his own feet. The girl shouted something after him. Her friends said something. Laird's feet hit the pavement and kept going, heart and brain driving a smart beat to which he walked like a man in a hurry, but not running.

He took out his phone and called Stephen. Hubert answered.

'Hubert, I'm sorry,' said Laird, 'but I'm lost. Someone, a student I think, just gave me a shove. She was talking with her friends before that, but I didn't understand what they were saying.'

Hubert told Laird to find out which street he was on.

'The police station is close. Wait a moment, and I'll give you directions,' he said, 'We'll be there in fifteen minutes.'

'We don't need to make a report.'

'You should make a report.'

Laird heard Stephen in the background asking Hubert, in English, what the hell was going on.

*

In front of Stephen and Hubert, Laird had to describe how the girl ran up behind him and pushed him. The officer asked him if he had any bruises or other injuries.

'I'm fine, totally fine. She just gave me a start. A shock.'

The officer asked him where and when. Then he leaned forward over the counter and asked,

'Was she black?'

Laird couldn't answer.

'Was she black?'

He wished the police officer hadn't asked that.

'I know them, these young people. They are in the street, in the same neighbourhood where she – attacked you,' he said.

'Are they homeless? They had iPhones!'

'They were drinking?'

'Drinking, maybe smoking.'

'Okay,' said the officer. He didn't write anything down.

Stephen and Hubert sat with Laird for a minute on the plastic seats in the police station waiting room.

'I'm fine,' said Laird. 'This is stupid. We missed our reservation.'

'We'll get a taxi,' said Stephen, 'Let's just go to one of the diners near my place.'

Le Rapido was dimly lit, and Laird felt himself grow calmer as they sidled into a booth against the back wall. The waitress switched to English for him, and he ordered a sandwich and a bottle of wine for the three of them. He was worse than a tourist here, but he could still order the only decent bottle of vino they had on the menu. Stephen and Hubert spared him a real conversation. They sat across from each other and talked about films.

Laird finished eating first, and went to use the bathroom. He locked himself in one of the cubicles so that he could sit by himself and rest his face on his hands. He was embarrassed and he was tired.

When he emerged from the bathroom, Stephen was still chatting to Hubert. He smiled at them, and joined the waitress by the window. A woman in her sixties, she was watching another woman who was standing alone on the kerb across the street.

The woman was all in white: white trainers, white tights, a white dress, even gloves and a hat. From a distance her dress looked poofy, sticking out as though she was wearing petticoats. Actually she was holding white poly bags, loads of them, on either side of her body. The bags were packed with clothes and God knew what else. Grey hair stuck out from under her skip cap. She might have been waiting for a taxi, or for someone to pick her up, but she didn't stick out her arm to hail a car, and no one came. She stood with her toes over the edge of the kerb, looking into the oncoming traffic. Her mouth was moving. She was talking to the people waiting at the crosswalk beside her. None of them looked at her. She was talking to herself. Her make-up, dry circles of rouge, was visible from across the street.

'Ça c'est Plateau-Mont-Royal,' said the waitress.

She smiled at him. Was it a joke? So he laughed.

The waitress looked proud. Proud of her joke, surely – not of this mad character who'd gathered herself to wait on the kerb, while everybody else went home or went for dinner.

Stephen and Hubert were silent now, watching Laird and the waitress. He went back to the table.

'I know you were keen to go to that restaurant,' said Stephen.

Laird could see in his son's face that he was worried, not knowing what he was supposed to say or do for his father, who hadn't cried since his last fight with John. Stephen knew some of those stories.

'It doesn't matter,' said Laird, 'We can go there next time I'm in town.'

'Good thinking Batman.'

'No, you and Hubert are Batman and Robin,' said Laird. He wasn't sure what that meant, after he said it.

'We can both be Robin,' said Hubert.

Alison Flett

EASTER
Adelaide, SA

Days pass.
Delicate skies.
Brittle sunlight.

The pardalote
on the path outside my house
crumples slowly in on itself:

feathers loosen and lift;
inner solids turn to liquid, to gas;
skin dips – a sling of flesh – a palimpsest.

Now there is only
the quiet web of bones,
the thin yellow cold

that clatters through them
and a slow persistent
tapping:

the egg tooth inside me
working away
at the self's   fragile   shell.

Graham Fulton

HOME FIXTURE

Jimmy Johnstone
      in Uddingston.

    A garden amongst the semi-detached
clippered hedges, numbered bins.
A throw-in from
      the slow food shop,
open *Morning*
        Noon and
          Night.

Wee Man statue. Strip of bronze.
      Sleeves rolled up, socks rolled down.
    Punching the sky. A football Earth
      beneath his boot, round and round,
    year after year, dribbling for peanuts.
League. Cup. Kick. Goal.
The same, then
        the same,
           again.
Everything, nothing.
Humanly perfect.
      Sculpted from something
older than sense.
The right to be pointless. Poet assassin.
      Ginger predator. 5 foot 2.
A god of flesh
at 3 p.m.

Benches to watch him.
        Standing stones.
Little floodlights
for evening worship.
Dreggy litter, 12 inch pizza boxes
Freshly Prepared For You.
Stamped-on cans of lager and beer.

A china plate on top of some slugs,
    dishwasher safe,

    a 7
on his shorts.

It's not his face. His hair's too old.
He looks like a tribune from ancient Rome.

        Jinky is dead.
      Paradise dust.
   Here are today's
league results.
   Here are today's
cup results.

As I leave I gather the junk age crap,
      spill some *Tennent's*
onto my shoe.

Charlie Gracie

from GERALDINE
(Excerpt from a novel-in-progress)

Chapter 1

The very moment Geraldine died, three distant Vs of geese flew past, skimming the edge of the city. April sat back in the chair. She looked out over the Vancouver skyline and smiled.

'That's you Mum. Thank you.'

Geraldine's eyes were closed. Her breathing had been shallow and soft for three days, but erupted in two long bursts before she passed on. April had laughed. 'What are you like!'

She looked over to her mother lying still on the bed, the pale flush of death beginning to set on her face. 'Out of the world in a big blast.'

Then she watched the geese arrive from Alaska for the easier winter on Vancouver Island. If Geraldine were awake ... alive, she would be telling April now about the geese coming in to Leitrim and Donegal for the winter. From Russia and Greenland. How they swept across in an arc from Donegal Bay, as if they had been swung round from Tory Island and pinged back onto the land at Killybegs.

At Kinlough, the geese, Brent and the occasional White Fronted, filled the flat fields below Arroo Mountain and Truskmore. The hilltops were flat too, flat hats above enormous rises of crag.

'I love the shapes of the land,' her mother had said. She could not understand how other people could not want to know every inch of this place.

Geraldine drew maps. At first, in London, she illustrated the parks of city and the rambles on the South Downs for a specialist retailer; quirky, yet recognisable, her artwork was so engaging that it became collectable. Later, when they moved to Canada, she drew for tourists: the Algonquin Park and Vancouver Island and the Columba River, where the geese would sift the wet edges for food.

April sat on. No point, she thought, in bothering the nurses now. With nothing left to do but feel for a pulse and confirm death.

She stood and looked out over the city. The light began to fade, Vancouver pulsing gently to life. She loved it here. Her home.

When the door opened, a nurse in a blue top and white trousers asked quietly, 'How is she?'

*

In the street, later, she found a quiet doorway and phoned Andy. She needed to talk to someone who made her feel safe and centred. He was the only person in her life now who did that. That fact made fear rise in her. Even when he asked if she wanted to meet up and she said 'yes, totally. I'd love it,' she kept a bit of the fear there, like a brake.

In the bar, she was glad to be with him. He listened, held her hand, smiled. Perhaps she could find a way to love him properly now, she thought.

Death then sex. It was not something that she thought would happen. After the drinks and a late supper, he was back at hers and nothing could stop the flow of the night. Grief to pleasure to sleep. This was only the third time they had slept together in her house. No light, on this occasion, from Geraldine's connected apartment; the 3 a.m. guilt flicker Andy had called it the first time.

'She's only worried,' April said.

'You're only nearly fifty.'

That was true. She laughed when he said it, but it was true. She was on a leash. She loved her Mum, but she was difficult.

'Is he married?' she looked April square in the eye. More Irish-sounding in these exchanges; a sudden tightness about her face.

'No, Mum. How could even ask that?'

She was so mad at her.

'And anyway, I am forty-seven years of age. Not your baby any more. Remember! If he is married, that's my worry, not yours.'

He was not married. He had been, but divorced ten years before April met him. She was the first woman that took his heart, he said.

'You just snuck in one day and stayed.'

'I think you held the door open quite wide for me, Andy.'

'True.' He smiled his half smile. He looked into the distance when he did that and it took her months to know that he was not dreaming of somewhere else or someone else, but thinking about her and him.

April struggled with commitment. How could she give her all to a man when she had a career like hers? And a mother like hers? How could she share the pressures around?

Geraldine did not help.

'No man will want to be bothered with a strong woman, April, so you have to decide what you want; a man or a job. That's what I did and look how well we're getting along.'

April did not say out loud that the occasional fuck might have helped her Mum's view of life. That's what she had with Andy; not, as she had hoped, occasional and uncomplicated; just far too occasional.

Before she slept, she pressed herself tightly onto his chest, just as he softened inside her. She squeezed her knees around him. She wanted to keep the moment for as long as she could.

'Am I staying tonight?'

'Damn right.' She looked into his eyes, soft-focussed. 'You're going to do this again in the morning before I throw you out the door...'

'Like an old dog?'

'No!' She laughed. 'Like a big, bad man.' She stroked his face with the back of her hand and felt him tighten in her again.

When she did waken in the first flicker of the morning, Andy was standing, already dressed beside her bed. He laid a tray on the table with apple juice and toast and a pot of coffee.

'In place of sex,' he said. 'You were so deep, just didn't want to spoil it for you.'

She closed her eyes and stretched, the softness of the morning seeping into her. Andy was looking at her when she opened her eyes again.

'Like a lioness,' he said.

'I feel fucking wrung out.'

'No wonder. Your mother just died. And all that shit with your work.'

'And a night of torrid sex.' She held her hand out to him.

'Yeah, that too.' He looked pleased with himself. Quite right too, she thought.

She got up and took the tray through to the living room. On the wall was a map of the five central royal parks of London. It was the original Geraldine had drawn when she was pregnant with April. She told her it took six of the nine months she carried her to complete.

The greens of Kensington Gardens and Hyde Park were contrasted with the soft purples of Green Park and St James's Park and, to the north, the tepid blue of Regent's Park. Geraldine had picked out the mood of each space and swept the buildings up like fallen leaves and scattered them round the whole of the city. April could nearly hear the music and the laughter of the sixties her mum described in her stories; she could almost smell the weed and feel the energy.

The map was stretched on a board and hung on the wall of the dining space they had shared together. At dinner, for the more than twenty years they had lived in the house, Geraldine held forth on the goings on of her friends and fellow artists. She was no slouch when it came to money, however, no Bohemian philanthropist.

'You have only yourself to sort, April. A few pound in your pocket is a good thing, but a few grand in the bank is a lot better.' She smiled, held her hand. 'We are women in this world with no man to hold us hostage with their bankbooks.'

Andy was there at dinner one night when her mother said that. After, he was angry.

'She has a fucking cheek sometimes.' He looked at her, intensely. 'You don't think like that do you?'

It was only then that April decided she would not think like that, open up a bit more. That was nearly four years earlier. Things had gone slowly since; not helped by Geraldine's descent into ill health.

April loved looking at the big map. It made her forget her mother's harshness and reminded her that she was a woman of substance, a creative, wonderful person; with a few rough edges that had never quite been smoothed out.

She stood there, sipping her coffee. Andy's arms squeezed round her waist; safe, strong arms. She leaned her head back against him, the smell of coffee mingling with his deodorant, the bitter coffee, the sweet smell of him.

'I love you.'

He said it quietly, like a fisherman teasing the fly on the surface of the river, gently so as not frighten the salmon.

'I love you.' Again.

April said nothing. She squeezed her head against him and smiled to herself.

'You trying to take advantage of me because I am grieving?'

'No.'

He turned her round by the shoulders and took the coffee cup from her hand.

'I want us to be together.'

He meant it; she knew that.

'I … need time. Still.'

He said nothing more, only placed the coffee cup back in her hand and kissed her on the forehead.

She turned back to the map of the Royal Parks. When she heard the door click shut, she wept.

George Gunn

AT SKIRZA

At Skirza there is a Norse midden full of cod bones & appetite
beside it there undoubtedly was a long hall
in there the skald Bragi Boddason would have stood
& told a tale from across the sea where words
like pine sap turn to amber in the mouths of storytellers
where cattle were grazed by the seacoast in Winter
& on the high pastures with the women in Summer
he comes from that country those women he claims
he also claims that a good saga takes two days
in telling & so he did standing in front of the fire
& no-one moved until the tale was over
& Bragi sat down & was given ale & meat & silence
'I come from across the sea' he said & it was true
because before them he had built a ship of poetry
from invisible nails rivets & planks
he had fashioned oak pine & ash
from this & other worlds & I tell you this
here now standing on a mound of knowledge
where the Sea is offered up & put into the Earth at Skirza

Mark Harding

REMOTE

Soccer Dad

Kim watched Mahmoud play soccer with the kids in the town square. She was at a discreet distance of two miles, too high to be seen or heard. Mahmoud broke off to wave to his right. A two-second delay while Kim's instruction bounced off the satellite to the drone: the camera panned across. Kim recognised Jasmin's blue hijab. Zoom out. The family setting off home. Mahmoud holding hands with his two boys. He may have been on the suspects list, but at least he spent time with his kids.

*

'Family life?' asked the psych assessor.

'Don't you people ever read your predecessor's reports? Divorced two years ago.' It hadn't hurt Kim that John had blamed her job. What hurt was that he never visited. Her boys needed a dad.

'And the job? Would you say the stress has got better?'

'Worse. As I said last time. In the old days, for a kill mission, I'd have a General on the IM. Nowadays it's almost done by post-it. Dammit, the President himself used to make the hard calls. Now we've expanded missions it's just …' She shrugged. Kim wondered what she'd wanted to say: too routine, too big, too 'efficient'?

'Why did you sign up to fly drones?'

'You should know by now the correct military term is Remotely Piloted Aircraft. Because it was cool.' Kim smiled weakly. 'And I was good at *Medal Of Honor.*'

*

Starry Night

Dayshift local time: night-time over the operations zone. On hot nights Mahmoud's family sometimes slept on the roof. Through thermal, Kim looked down on the huddle of the boys and, slightly apart, Mahmoud and Jasmin. The two shapes merged into one, making love, under the stars and the drones.

*

End of the shift, and Kim was in a rush to pick up the boys from school, but she had to read and sign yet another procedure notice on computer viruses. Each time the penalties for bringing flash drives onto the base grew more severe. It was the S-Virus causing the panic, of course. Apparently it had disabled half the Chinese Air Force. All the pilots agreed it was typical of IT to imply they were the risk. IT hardly had a good track record. Luckily previous infections hadn't been harmful, whereas this one ... well, Kim didn't like to think about what you should call it.

*

Working Late

Mahmoud often went out with his uncle's mobile clinic, returning home after dark. Two miles to go, and the vehicle pulled over. Kim got a hazy thermal image of the bodies inside, and a clearer image of the man who'd stepped out to take a piss. It was probably Mahmoud, he seemed to be having bladder problems lately. Kim hoped his uncle would notice, or Jasmin would make sure Mahmoud got it checked out.

*

When she saw the kill list, Kim expected the error to be corrected immediately. Probably another case of Intelligence mixing up two unfamiliar names.

Kim checked with the other pilots. They confirmed Mahmoud was spotless, not even red flags on the phone monitoring.

She IM'd this to NCOM, with a request for target confirmation.

Two minutes later, for the first time in months or even longer, she got a phone call from a colonel.

'You got a problem?'

'No sir,' Kim replied.

'Good, I don't have time for problems.'

'I was just, uh, just trying to avoid any accidents, sir.'

'You recognize we have intelligence sources other than RPAs?'

'Yes, sir.'

'Do you need an extra psych assessment?'

'No, sir!'

*

The School Run

It hadn't surprised Kim to be assigned the strike. In the military, destiny had a talent for sick jokes.

She tailed Mahmoud's battered Honda from a height of fifteen thousand feet, an easy task when you knew the car so well. The school roadside was full of parked cars, so Mahmoud stopped mid-road. A boy jumped out and ran into the grounds. Mahmoud drove on. Where was the other son?

Kim IM'd NCOM.

The response was immediate:

> **Collateral risk noted. Cleared to attack.**

The execution point was a small café where Mahmoud ate breakfast before driving out to the clinic. Orders were to fire while he was in the car to minimise casualties. But now Kim hesitated.

Mahmoud still hadn't got out. Dealing with the child?

Kim positioned, textbook. She wiped the sweat from her eyes. Failing to shoot now, would mean more casualties later. She launched the missile. Or tried to. Her RPA veered aside and weapons went cold. Dumbfounded, she tried again. Same thing.

Kim ran diagnostics. The drone's report was unexpected:

    } **Safety First! People could get hurt.**

    : **U read this?** She IM'd to NCOM.

    > **Hold position.**

A long silence. The phone chirped. A junior tech, too fraught to be embarrassed, wanted to know if her drone's computer contained a copy of the old missile control software, from six years ago.

'Don't you keep backups?' Kim exclaimed.

'Going back six years? The S-virus infected the manufacturer, lying dormant. It's in the weapons system of every drone we know.'

'Okay, I'll look.'

The diagnostics link was sluggish, the drone's onboard files were slow to list. Kim wondered who'd written the virus, how they'd been able to spread it. There! The old weapons software, six years old. She could restore the archive file and get the team back to kill-ready. She could complete her mission.

Kim highlighted the file.

And deleted it.

A mile below the drone, Mahmoud got out the car and lifted his boy into his arms.

Gail Honeyman

DOLORES READS A CALFSKIN JOURNAL

When I found his journal, I just *knew*. He thinks he's so smart, so terrifically intellectual, but *of course* he was going to drone on in a fancy-schmancy prose style, and *of course* it was going to be all about how much he loved me, and what a swell guy he was for loving me, and how ungrateful I was. He was in the bathroom when I found it, taking a long shower, singing some sappy song in French – it was so corny, the tune, that you'd think he'd be embarrassed that someone could hear him. Not him, though. He's beyond embarrassment, knows no shame.

When we arrived at this motel, he locked the door behind us and pocketed the room key before we'd even unpacked, like he always does. I looked around, like I always do, but the windows didn't open, and the view was just the usual deserted lot, with the trash cans and, this time, a sad little cat. It was half heartedly washing its face, didn't even look up when an empty soda can toppled from the garbage and rattled around on the asphalt. Like the last place, there was no phone in this crummy dump. Not that it mattered – times when there was one, he'd pull the cord from the wall.

Afterwards, and after all the usual afterwardsy stuff, he said nothing, just looked at me and smirked as he got up from the bed, took the room key from the night stand and went off into the bathroom with it, humming. Yet again, I was forced to watch his saggy back and his flabby arms disappear, taking with them my only means of escape, and then I had to just lie around and wait and wait and wait.

He thinks that I lack imagination, that I'm dumb, my mind's *pedestrian*. I read that in his journal, but it was only telling me what I already knew. So I don't enjoy artichokes, or Balzac or Dürer (although, truthfully, I loved those engravings, especially that hare). So shoot me. Just because I prefer comic books and movies and jiving, that doesn't mean I'm stupid. At the end of the day, *he's* the dummy, for not realising what a boring old phoney he is, and that he's way behind the times. There's no point in trying to tell him, trying to talk to him about anything, though, because he won't listen to me. Sure, he knows more than me about a heap of stuff, but that's only because he's been alive for longer.

It's actually one of the worst things (I won't be writing down the very worst things) about this crazy setup. I can never be the one who gets to show him anything, can't ever introduce him to something new, or explain stuff. As far as he's concerned, he's already done it, or seen it, or thought it, or been it. That's not because he's smart and I'm dumb, though. It's because he's thirty-seven, and I'm twelve and a half.

So, I'm sitting here listening to him singing, the water from the shower pitpattering against the bathtub, and I can smell the soapy steam escaping under the gap at the bottom of the bathroom door, all lemony. He sounds really happy. There's a radio on the dresser, and I turn it on. I turn the music up loud, loud enough to drown him out (the next best thing, since I can't actually drown him ... jeez, that's the kind of lame joke that *he* would make).

I read the whole thing while he's been in there, and then I decided that I should start writing things down too, including plenty of mean stuff about him, since he's put a whole heap in about me. I can start this afternoon because, once he's finally out of the shower, he'll still need to floss, shave, buff his nails and trim all that horrible hair (ears, nose, down below – urgh) with tiny scissors. He's always saying that it's important to be *meticulous in one's twah-let.* For someone who spends so much time in the bathroom, he sure smells bad sometimes.

I don't know how long the notepaper will last out today – way too much of it is taken up already with the heading, *Shady Nooks Motel,* and the address and phone number. At the foot of the page it says *Pleasure awaits you in Shady Nooks.* Huh. Everywhere we've stayed has had stationery. We've stayed in some swanky places, and some dives, and they've all provided it. Until my darling stepdaddy took me on this trip, I hadn't so much as had brunch in a hotel (*an* hotel, he always says – pompous ass) and now I must have stayed in, oh, hundreds. In hotel rooms, I've sometimes wanted to drink a glass of soda, or lie in the tub and scrub my skin till it looks like raw meat, or to scream and scream until someone saved me or I died from screaming, but I've never felt the urge to write a letter. The things that go on in our hotel rooms are not the kind of things you'd want to write about, and anyways, he's told me what he'll do to me if I ever think about telling anyone.

But who'd I write to, if I even wanted to send a letter? My mother is dead – so *he* says, anyway – and I don't have anyone else. He's my family now. Back at the start, I tried to leave a note, wrote down the number plate of his dirty old car and some basic details and PLEASE SEND HELP, but he noticed it sticking out from under the mattress, and now he sweeps the room before we leave. Every time, checking everywhere. He's not as smart as he thinks he is, but he's too damn good at finding stuff like that, and at second guessing me.

I've put the journal back in his *vah-leeze*, but he'll probably know that I've read it. I'm pretty sure, now I think about it, that he wanted me to read it – he'd have found a smarter hiding place otherwise, and he doesn't check I'm really asleep before he takes it out at night. Just the sight of it reminds me how much I hate him. Reason: most folks just have a diary, something normal, plain, bought in a store. Not him, though. He has a *journal*, shiny yellow lettering on the front and spine, stamped with his initials (HH – like golden prison gates). It's bound in blood red calfskin.

It's a word I've heard before, but today I've thought about it, really thought about it, and realised that it's not a made up term. Calfskin is really, truly, the actual skin of a baby cow. Imagine it: one day, a calf was taken from its mother against its will, and they never saw each other again. Then the little calf had its skin sliced off, peeled back from its bones, dried and dyed red. The dead baby calf's slicked off skin ends up wrapped around this book of his. I've seen him stroking it, when he thinks I'm asleep.

So the outside of the journal gives me nightmares, but the words inside make me furious. One of the latest things he's written, after all these months travelling around, all those miles, is this:

We had been everywhere. We had really seen nothing.

How can he say that? We've worked our way through the first big chunk of the *Guide to These United States;* cotton candy factories, enchanted forests, Indian reserves, a petting zoo. That day was terrific. I got to hold a chubby koala bear, rub its tufty ears and listen to it snuffling. It felt really warm, and weighed surprisingly heavy in my arms. The keeper told me lots of cool stuff, about how their babies are called joeys, and how koalas are one of the few other animals to have fingerprints. They look just like ours, he told me – if you inked my thumb and that little grey bear's, and then rolled them both onto a sheet of paper, when you looked at the two prints side by side, you'd struggle to tell the difference. I said that if I ever committed a crime, I'd be sure to look for a koala bear to pin it on, and the man laughed, ruffled my hair and told me I was one heck of a cute kid. He didn't stroke my hair, or wind it round his finger, he just quickly ruffled it. It felt good. Of course, *he* came right over, started asking the keeper all these dumb ass questions, like was it true that most of the koalas over in Australia were riddled with some dirty disease, laughing too loud. No one else laughed. I buried my face in the koala's fur, wished I could crawl into its pouch and stay there forever.

Oftentimes, these places have a gift store, and that's always my favourite part of the visit. They'll carry souvenir erasers, or these really neat jumbo pencils with the name of the place down the side. Sometimes you can buy dime-sized lapel buttons, and they almost always have postcards on a squeaky stand you can twirl as you decide which ones to buy. When we first set off on this journey, he'd buy me heaps of gifts, stuff I asked for and even stuff I hadn't. After two or three months, though, he started a system where he makes me earn them. I have to think hard about it now, about how much I really want a dreamcatcher or some bangles. He says that I'm greedy, *mercenary*, and he gets ticked off that we have to go shopping after I've done what he wants. He doesn't enjoy the gift stores, says they're *tedious*, and *tawdry*, and that most of the goods are in *lamentably bad taste*.

One time, he flat out refused to buy me this cool plastic pineapple (this was in one of the Museums of Canned Produce, I can't remember which one), said the thing was a *monstrosity, beyond the pale, offensive*. This was after I'd done the thing he'd asked me to, and let him do the other things, in the parking lot. I got so mad, I started to scream at him, then before he could stop me I got out of the car and kicked it as hard as I could, yelling that it was SO UNFAIR and he was a MEAN OLD MAN! Some woman was walking by, pushing a baby in a stroller, and he clamped his hand over my mouth, started shoving me into the passenger seat, pinching my arm with his free hand.

The lady was staring at us, looking really serious, and I was thinking that, finally, this might be it. Then he started telling her what a challenge teenage girls were, and how they all rebel at this stage and have these dreadful temper tantrums, and wasn't she lucky to have a bouncing baby boy – *adorable*. He hoped she'd enjoy these magical early years before adolescence arrives and the hormones take over. By the end of all this, I'd been shoved inside, and locked in the car. I sat there, staring at the dashboard, just listening as she laughed, wished him luck, told him that he wasn't to worry, that I'd grow out of it soon and blossom into a charming young woman, she was sure. It's like I said – old people are dummies.

I can hear him coughing now; he's turned off the shower so I don't know how much longer I'll have to write this. I just want enough time to note down what happened yesterday. It wasn't so very different than any other day, I guess. They all feel pretty much the same now, and I don't know if it's Wednesday or Sunday, or how long it is till Thanksgiving. I guess it's because we don't live in a house, and there's no school anymore. I'm no brainiac, but I'd give anything for a pile of homework now, for my mother to be yelling at me to come inside and finish my assignment.

So, we left the motel early yesterday – I can't remember the name of it, or the colour of the walls, or what I ate for breakfast. I can only usually remember them if there's something really different, like a fish tank in the lobby. There was one, somewhere, that had these amazing clown fish with bulgy eyes. The lady let me feed them, and I sprinkled the grey flakes onto the surface and then watched as the fish gently kissed them down. There was one in Arkansas where a white west highland terrier lived in Reception, and snoozed all day on a plaid blanket.

Anyways, this had been one of the blah places, and I was glad to be moving on. In bed that morning, he'd told me to look through the guidebook, and I'd found us a scenic mountain viewpoint not too far away, headed in the right direction, that sounded pretty awesome. He wasn't keen, but in the end he usually takes me where I want to go.

When we arrived, it was lovely – there was a ritzy little coffee stand with seating outside. The weather was warm, soft but with a hint of a chill in the wind, like the absolute end of summer. It was busy, packed with visitors. I love it when there are lots of other people around. We sat at one of the rustic benches, and he bought us some coffee and two hot donuts each for lunch. I remember I had a moustache and beard of sugar all round my mouth afterwards, and I licked the grains off, running my tongue over and around my lips, liking the scratchy feel of them. Too late, I realised he was staring at me, in *that* way, and I swiped the back of my hand across my mouth, wiping it on my skirt to get rid of the rest.

We wandered up to the viewpoint, not talking, and leaned over the rail. Everything was hazy – smoky blue mountains, a heat shimmer, and a drop that I wouldn't even know how to measure. It was like we were at the very top of the world. I didn't feel anything much. He put his arm around my shoulders as we looked, and he drew tiny circles on my upper arm with his big sausage fingers. After a minute or two, we turned around, with our backs to the view and all the nice stuff behind us, facing forwards like someone was going to take a photo.

Some people were having a picnic not far from where we stood, and I could see a blanket spread out over the grass, and a wicker basket filled with muffins, sandwiches and fruit. There was a Thermos, family sized, and bottles of soda – they hadn't eaten yet, by the looks of things. The mother was lying on her side on the blanket, her head propped up on her arm, and she was laughing at something the father said. He was pouring coffee into a cup, which he then placed in front of her, and kissed the top of her head. There were two kids right behind them, playing tennis. They weren't very good, and the girl flunked every shot. The boy wasn't angry – he was laughing at her but you could tell it wasn't the nasty kind of laughter, because she was laughing too. I screwed up my eyes against the sun, realising that there was something really familiar about these people, trying to think what it was. I felt him shift and stiffen beside me – jeez, how does he manage to know everything I'm thinking?

The McCrystals! I asked him, pleaded with him, offered to do anything and everything, anytime, if we could just go over, talk to them for a minute or two. I was whispering, tugging at his arm, begging him. The McCrystals! Cherry was a big, clumsy girl, kind of dumb and not at all popular. Her brother Brandon was two years younger, and everyone said he'd gone to the bathroom in his pants when the fire alarm went off that one time. But oh, the McCrystals, here! He said no, of course, marched me back down the slope to the parking lot in double quick time, told me to stop snivelling and gave me his big handkerchief to blow my nose on once we were back inside the car.

Onwards, he said, putting the damp handkerchief back in his pocket, running his fat finger down the list of accommodation in the guidebook to see where we'd be heading. I took the book from him, placed it in my lap. My throat was sore from crying, but I swallowed and tried to speak as clearly as I could. I said to him, tell me this, honestly, because I have to know – what did I ever do to deserve any of this?

He smiled. He smiled! Oh my Lolita, my luscious little Lo, he said. Please don't question why I love you, or whether you deserve my love. Know only this: to me, you are the blue and green world and the infinite expanse of the heavens. You are my moon, my stars, and my bright little sun. Divine, celestial Lolita!

Sheer and total one hundred per cent baloney. He smiled at me again, took hold of my hand, waited for me to say something. I said nothing. He stroked my cheek, and I tried not to flinch, because it makes him angry. It's better not to make him angry. At the end of the day, there's only the two of us, and I've got nowhere else to go. He asked me why I wasn't saying anything, and I shrugged. He said that perhaps he hadn't expressed himself appropriately. He said he'd put it another way, easier to understand. You, my pet, are a dazzling red balloon, made from air and light, and I'm the string, joined to you, letting you fly, gazing up to admire you as you dance through soft summer breezes. I nodded, he started the car and we drove off. I know what you did to my balloon, mister, I thought.

So that was yesterday. We moved on, and we keep moving on. I don't know what the future holds, how long we'll keep going. One day, when I'm really old, maybe twenty or so, what I'd like is to meet a nice guy, go steady. Marry, eventually, with no fuss, no witnesses. We'll live in a cosy little house with smoke coming out of the chimney, have a cat and a dog and a bird. Nothing fancy: no *boeuf bourguignon*, no poetry. My boy will be someone quiet, hardworking, good with his hands – a carpenter, maybe. That's what I'd like. Two babies, maybe three. A little garden for them to play in.

The notepaper's nearly done, and I can hear him finishing up in the bathroom. If had more paper, and more time, this is what I'd write, until there was no paper left in the world or my hand fell off.

Let me go, let me go, let me go.

Repeat until the page is full, printer.

Alison Irvine

THE NOTE

Emma was determined to get the nappy on this time, despite the kicking legs and twisting hips, so with her toddler's ankles in one hand and a nappy in the other she heard but ignored the note as it was posted through the door. Mark was away for a greyfriar's bobby as he'd told her so sweetly ten minutes previously which meant that neither of them could have opened the door and chased after whoever had written the note had they wanted to, which they would have, had they known what they would read.

Emma released her bare-legged baby. She was off, tottering on eighteen-month-old legs towards the walls, the door, the corner of the table, and all the other hazards in the house. She fell over the carpet and stayed on her hands and knees, nappied bum in the air, head on the floor.

'Are you tired, Mia?' Emma said.

'No.'

Emma stood up, tucked the heel of her foot into her slipper and righted her daughter, setting her down on her feet and giving her head a stroke.

'Daddy,' Mia said and trundled to the bathroom door slapping her hands against it.

'I'm doing a jobby!' Mark shouted.

'Daddy!'

'Give me a minute!'

Emma opened the bathroom door and let Mia in. She saw Mark put down his paper and reach for the toilet roll.

Emma was furious and tired. Mark had confessed that morning that he'd been awake during one of Mia's night-time episodes. Up down, up down, cry cry, mummy, mummy, twinkle twinkle, got a sheep baa baa, on and on and on.

'You were awake? Why didn't you help me then?'

'I'd have been doing it wrong.'

'What?'

'She doesn't respond to me. She just wants her mummy and cries more.'

'You were awake and you didn't help. Arsehole.'

*

She walked past the note on the floor in the hall, forgetting its existence, intent on boiling the kettle and spending as much as forty seconds without anybody placing a single demand on her.

When Mark joined her in the kitchen he held, away from Mia's swiping hands, the note.

'You have to read this. It's not a joke.'

Mia lunged for the paper and nearly tipped herself out of Mark's arms.

'Good god, she's strong,' he said.

Mia cried, rubbed her eyes and reached for Emma.

'Oh baby,' Emma said. 'Oh baby, you are tired.'

Mark tried to pass Mia to Emma but Mia turned herself into his chest, tucking up her knees and curling into him.

'I'll rock her in the pram,' Emma said. 'I'll drink my tea when it's cold.'

'I'll get it, you read this.'

Mark passed their hot-cheeked child to Emma, along with the note. Happy to be in her mother's arms, Mia poked at Emma's face saying 'eyes, nose, hair' while Mia read.

> *To the occupants of flat 2:1*
>
> **Re: Last night, and other nights.**
>
> *If you intended to keep the whole building awake while your baby cried, you achieved your goal. SELFISH! Change your method of getting her to sleep. Leaving her to cry does not work.*
>
> *Yours,*
>
> *Sleepless in Wishart Road.*

Emma's first reaction was to defend her daughter, to say, indignantly, that she wasn't that bad. But she was, she was awful.

She said, 'Mark,' on the verge of tears and held up the note. Mark was setting up the pram in the hall. They shared a look that combined shock and defiance all at once and despite her deep (and almost perpetual) anger at him, during that look she found him handsome and heroic. He was the barefoot and bed-headed twenty-seven-year-old who stood in her kitchen singing 'Freedom Come All Ye' and not the sleep-deprived thirty-seven-year-old on a precarious contract with a bad back and a, let's be frank, partner tipping between hysteria and despair-drenched exhaustion.

Emma lowered Mia into the pram. Mia stretched her legs, arched her back and squawked.

'Who do you think wrote it?' Mark said as Emma fastened the straps and lowered the backrest with a jerk.

'Sorry baby, you weren't ready for that were you?'

Mia cried, reached a hand to Emma's face and then her little fist went back to her eyes.

'Let me get her to sleep, then we'll talk about it.' She began to rock the pram.

'I'm staggered.'

'So am I.'

'Who do you think it was?'

'Mamamamamama.'

'Mark, she won't sleep if she hears us talking,' Emma hissed. 'Turn the light off.'

Did he huff? Was she being a control freak? She was too tired to care.

She rocked and sang and rocked and sang. Mark watched, holding the note. Emma wanted to tell him to do something – the recycling, the dishes, anything – but she knew she would be a confirmed control freak if she did. And also, he held the note.

'Has she gone off yet?'

Mark checked. 'Nearly.'

Emma began another verse and chorus of Allyballybee.

'No name or flat number,' Mark said, pointing to the note.

'Cowards,' Emma whispered.

'Well there must be at least two cowards because the note says *us*. "Keeping *us* awake."'

Emma's rocking speeded up. Mia changed position in the pram, rolling onto her side, always a good sign that she was about to go.

'It's the controlled crying isn't it?' Emma said. 'You were right, we shouldn't have done it.'

'It wasn't that long.'

'It was last night. You were asleep. Or you said you were. Oh God.'

Night-times were hard because Emma and Mark wanted different things. Mark wanted sleep and Emma did want sleep yet all those books, those bloody books, told her one thing and another and stressed how important it was not to feed her milk or let her in bed with them. And what did Mark say when he intervened, if he intervened? 'Give her a bottle for God's sake' or 'Just stick her in with us. Night night.'

And inevitably, Emma would feed the baby or stick her in with them and wish she'd done it an hour ago. So the night before, she'd tried leaving Mia to settle herself, closing her eyes to her baby's cries and counting two, three, five, seven, ten minutes each time before she went back into her room. It hadn't worked.

'Maybe they had a job interview today,' Mark said.

'On a Saturday? Fuck them.'

Mark picked up the note. 'It's not even hand-written.'

'Typists.'

'Cunts.'

Emma loved it when Mark swore as much as she did.

At last Mia slept and sweet Jesus, the quiet, the peace. The little jump inside her when she saw her daughter sleeping, a face full of cheeks and eyelashes. And oh God, the relief of letting out that held-in pee.

Pee over, something had to be done about the note.

'Right! Okay then!' Emma shoved her cup of tea into the microwave. 'I'm going door knocking. I'll shame them. Whoever it is, they can see me like this; ugly, tired, on the edge, and realise their note has just about tipped me over into insanity. Is my hair too greasy?'

Mark glanced up from the dishes. 'No,' he said, and Emma saw something like pity in his face. Highly likely she thought, ran a brush through her hair, had a quick gulp of tea, and pulled the door quietly behind her.

Her neighbours in the ground floor flats denied writing the note. The woman with the dog said, yes, she sometimes heard crying, but she'd brought up two of her own on her own so knew what it was like. Emma left before she cried.

Across from their own front door, Emma knocked on the house of the couple with the teenage girls. Nobody home. She walked up the stairs and looked out at the back courts with their washing lines and rain-soaked bin sheds. When Mark got his new job, the one he had now, with the evening obligations and renewable short-term contract, he told Emma he didn't miss the flat, that in hindsight he'd spent a little too long at the windows watching the comings and goings of people he'd never met or hardly knew. I used to get obsessed with turning the lights off, he told her once. And Emma understood, now that she'd gone back to part-time hours, because it frightened her to think of who she was only a few months ago, alone in the house and under siege.

She went on up the stairs to the flat directly above them. The man opened his door. A face full of wrinkles. Black hair. Bare feet. Attractive, Emma thought, and was surprised by the peculiarly inappropriate return of her libido.

'Hello neighbour,' he said. 'We're watching television.' He opened the door for her to step inside.

'I got this note,' she said and held it out for him.

He took it and read it.

'You think we wrote it.'

'I'm asking everyone.'

He called out, 'Mary!'

Emma followed the man through to his living room where an electric fire blazed and the blinds were closed. Emma saw the man's wife kneeling in front of the television, her blond, unmoved hair hanging down her back. She held a remote control in her hand and didn't stand up.

'Mary!'

The woman looked around and said with no smile, 'Do you like song and dance films?'

'Song and dance—?'

'*Annie Get Your Gun* was supposed to be on but I can't find it,' She turned wildly to her husband and said, 'there's definitely been a mistake with the listings. It's not on.'

'Are you sure?'

'I've been through all the channels and all the times. You'd better email the paper and tell them they've made another mistake.'

'Would it make you happy?'

'Yes, I think it would.'

Good Lord, Emma thought. Would it make you happy?

The man held out his hands to Emma, as if remembering she was in the room.

'How do you take your tea?'

'I can't stay …'

'Come on, we love a visitor.'

Emma sat on a chair at their square dining table. The placemats were purple. Two ceramic salt and pepper pot figures hugged. Emma touched a finger to their curves and looked up to see her neighbours staring at her.

'Oh yes, the note,' the man said, picking up the cups that were already on the table. 'It's Emma isn't it? She's getting harassed, Mary, by an anonymous note writer who doesn't like greeting babies.'

The woman stood up and smoothed her hair behind her neck and down one shoulder.

'We hear your baby,' she said.

'Yes. We do hear your baby and have a laugh about it – someone shut the little brat up – but we didn't write this note,' the man said and handed it to his wife who passed it, without looking, back to Emma.

Emma didn't like either of them. The brat word had sealed it. Mia was an exhausting, unsleeping yet loveable baby, not a brat. Only parents had the right to call their child a brat.

'I work from home,' the man's wife said to Emma. 'I used to see your husband from time to time.'

'My partner. We're not married.'

'I could hear him too. I used to think we should stop for lunch at the same time, as if we were proper workers in an office.'

'He wasn't working, he was looking for work.'

'Oh, how I'd love to watch movies all day.'

'I better go,' Emma said.

'But you haven't had your tea.'

'She doesn't have to have a cup of tea.'

The man ignored his wife. 'Tell me, while you're here, I wonder if we could get your opinion on something.

'No!' the woman said.

'I'll put the kettle on and then I'll be back.'

He left the room, in his bare feet, without a sound. And the woman pounced.

'He's round the bend. You don't have to agree with him. You don't even have to answer him. I don't. I never do.'

The woman had something in the corner of her mouth. Food. Toothpaste. Her face, close up, was frighteningly thin.

'Charming, isn't he? But you just take my lead,' she said and Emma thought she heard a cry, but Mia couldn't be crying so soon, she'd only just gone down. She had at least another forty-five minutes to go and in that time Emma needed to wash herself and some clothes and possibly the kitchen floor and the toilet and the bath.

The woman stood in the doorway then closed the door. Emma wondered if she stamped on the floor, would Mark come up and rescue her.

'I wrote the note,' the woman hissed at Emma.

'You wrote the note?'

'Don't tell him. Ignore it. I didn't mean what I said.'

'Why?'

'He'll punish me for it.'

She opened the door and called out for her husband, turning to Emma and putting a finger to her lips. She raised her eyebrows, playfully. Emma thought of Burton and Taylor, George and Martha, and wondered if every couple had its games.

The man returned with a newspaper.

'Spot the typo,' he said.

The woman cried out. 'Leave her alone!' She picked up the remote control, tidied away a newspaper, threw a cushion onto a chair.

'There's a typo in this article,' the man said.

'No, there isn't.'

'Read it. See if you can find it.'

'Leave her alone!'

His wife grabbed the paper. 'Please, not today,' she said but her husband snatched the paper from her and spread it out on the table.

'Read it and spot the typo.'

'You're a cunt,' said his wife.

'And I love you.'

'I don't love you.' The woman moved to the window and peered through the blinds.

The article was about a woman in court because she perjured herself at the trial of a former boyfriend.

'You'll see our Mary here is the woman in the dock.'

He slapped his hand next to a grainy picture of his wife. There was another picture of his wife and a man, the two of them near-naked under a beach parasol.

'I don't know if I should read this,' Emma said.

'Yes, you should. Read on. It gets lovely and seedy.'

Emma read about Mary, who stood in the dock and told Sherrif and jury that her boyfriend couldn't have stood outside the house of the ex who owed him money and threatened to pour petrol through her letter box because he was at home with her. And he couldn't have done it several times over the course of three months because he was with her each time. She could prove it. And when the house did go up in flames, he couldn't have done that either, because again, he was with her.

'You're jealous!' the woman shrieked from the window.

'But you know what, neighbour,' the man said, 'she lied. She lied! Poor Mary loved him so much she couldn't send him to prison so she lied. She told me she was frightened of what he would do. Poor little put-upon Mary.'

'You're as bad as him!'

'Was she immoral? That is the question. Was she weak and immoral? Yes she was.'

The woman moved back to the table and said quietly, 'Our neighbour wishes to leave. She's had enough of you.'

The electric fire flickered behind her.

The man took the article away. 'The long and the short of it is,' he said, 'after the fire, this woman tried to take her own life she was so desperate. And she nearly did kill herself, were it not for a neighbour who came round unexpectedly and found her. Apparently the neighbour wanted to put a note through the door to complain about the noise of the lady's children running amok but she knocked first and when there was no answer she had some kind of sixth sense and called for her son to help charge the door down. And they found her up to her eyeballs in paracetamol.'

The man put an arm around his wife.

'So Mary here is let off the hook. Not a murderer-by-proxy, just a liar.'

The woman said nothing.

'That's why you escape into your song and dance films, isn't it, to get away from yourself?'

'I hate you,' the woman said and she looked at Emma and any playfulness in her face was long gone.

Nobody spoke. The man appeared to have said all he wanted to say.

Eventually he said, 'Did you spot the typo?'

'No.'

'Are you sure?'

'I didn't read it closely,' Emma said.

'There is no typo,' the woman said. 'You can look and look but there is no typo.'

The man laughed.

'Poor Mary.'

'No, you are the poor one. I suffer you but you have to suffer yourself.'

And the woman stared at Emma with tears in her eyes, before picking up the remote control and turning back to the television.

Emma walked slowly down the stone close steps. The rain flicked against the landing window and it seemed not a soul was outside, all the walls

and roofs and lanes wet and empty. In her own house, the lights were on.
Mark and Mia were in the bedroom looking at picture books. Emma got
in bed beside them.

'I thought I'd sleep when she was sleeping,' Mark said. 'But she woke up.'

Emma picked up one of the books and felt a teddy's fluffy tummy, turned
a page and touched another teddy's shiny nose.

'Did you find out who wrote the note?'

Mia put a book in Emma's lap.

'It was the woman upstairs,' Emma said.

'What's that?' Mia said to Emma.

'A cow.'

'Did you give it to them Emma-style?'

'What's that?' Mia said.

'A sheep. No, I didn't.'

'Baa.'

'Why not?'

'What's that?' Mia said.

'It wasn't that kind of note in the end.'

'What's that?'

'They were offensive. Horrible. I can't work out if she's just crazy, or if
it was some kind of cry …'

'WHAT'S THAT?!'

'For help. A duck. A duck. A duck!'

'Quack.'

Emma turned to the book's first page and Mia climbed onto her lap.
Her daughter leaned back and Emma peered round her head and read the
words, her mouth grazing Mia's hair as she spoke.

'So what do we do about the note?' Mark said.

'Bin it,' Emma said. 'No, we should keep it, just in case something
really is wrong.'

'And the crying in the night?'

'Endure it, I guess. She'll sleep through eventually.' She squeezed
Mark's hand.

Emma told herself she would speak in detail with Mark later on, when
Mia was in the bath or in bed. She would attempt to describe the couple
upstairs and the newspaper article. Was Emma being fanciful? What did
the woman want her to do? Be her friend? Tell someone? Emma tried to
imagine what she would do if she was in trouble in her own house. Would
she send a note? But the more tired she got, as the days went on, the more

doubtful she felt as to what she could actually do anyway. She never heard anything from upstairs: no worrying noises, no arguments, barely a footstep, and when she did hear footsteps they sounded homely and safe.

It was only when Mia cried in the night that Emma's conviction came back with sudden and frightening clarity.

Brian Johnstone

DETAIL
The Falklands Conflict, 1982

They called a spade, a spade; a grave,
a grave; and duty unequivocal. His, to lead
the burial detail out to what the islanders
called camp. Body bags scarce, they laid them out
as if for night, each sleeping sack a winding sheet.

Too late, his flinch as the soil went in, the load
misaimed, the heft of his spade mistimed,
revealing the face of his mate below. Too late
to turn, too late to escape the stare that said,
I am not dead, even though he knew it was a lie.

They called a scare, a scare; a shock, a shock;
endurance indispensable. His, to yomp on
through the future, that face ever there: a friend
who never said to him, *Don't bury me*, but says it
every waking hour in all the trenches of his brain.

David Kinloch

LICHTUNG
(after **The Clearing** *by Andrew Wyeth)*

Everything is falling, pouring onto the switch-
grass and the Sweet Joe Pye Weed.

Shoulders cascade upon his torso and the tan line
pulls tight the stack of thighs.

Ferns bunch about his genitals, his cock a cut
above the avocado of his balls; his pubic hair

writhes up in streaks of luminescence. He glows
against the dark break of the conifers.

Behind, the sea is there and tiny zephyrs
still whirr about his long blond hair.

Arnold's stats compel the sheepish
copy of plain words and simple statements.

Here is Venus, rising from the back
pasture, his strong girl's face

insisting you receive him as he is.
Yes. He has a history: just yesterday

he slept with both boys by the riverside;
his Warhol screen test went up

in smoke and mirrors; he leapt
five stories down and was broken in.

The phosphorescence of his limbs
is the glitter of putrescence:

sand dollars, shiners dying as he rose.
His shell is wholly clear now

for this encounter.

Helen Lamb

THE GRANDMAS

The grandmas say ten fingers of gin,
a steaming bath,
leave the hot tap running until
I slither out
slick as calf's liver.

They say dislodge me,
it's not too late.
Hurl yourself down the steep stairs.
I am boneless.
You will mend.

Instead you clench around me,
a cage of muscle,
your heart drumming.
Your rebel blood
floods my cells.

You don't know yet
how hard I'll be to love
or who will do the soothing.
Who will help you count
my ten neat toes?

Marcas Mac an Tuairneir

INDIGO

I'm the dark dye of the Indies
And the blackness of soundless midnight.
I'm the depth of secrets
Overflowing in your veins.

I'm emblem of your heroism,
Brave dedication to your campaign.
I'm the tincture on your body
And the sharp shriek in your cacophony.

I'm the pounding of the leaves
Bitter, sticky to the marrow,
Like the pulp of your foe's gore
Lying pulsating on the battleground.

I'm the mark of your prosperity,
Undying under Mandinka fingernail.
I'm rebellion, as well,
And gushing blood-lust for Bengal.

My black seed symbolised oppression
For alien sake and wealthy exhibition
And I'm the mists and the ocean
Magellan navigated under sail.

Marcas Mac an Tuairneir

GUIRMEAN

Mise dath daor nan Innseachan
Is dubhachas mheadhan-oidhche chiùin.
Mise doimhneachd rùn dìomhair,
A' siubhal, taosgach, tro do chuislean.

Mise samhladh d'fheardhachd
Is misneachd shuisdealach den iomairt.
Mise lì-dhealbh air do bhodhaig
Is a' ghaoir gheur do ghliongraiche.

Mise prannadh nan duilleag
Sealbh is slaopach gu smior,
Mar phronnadh gaorr an nàmhaid,
Na laighe na phlosgadh san àraich.

Mise samhladh do shealbhmhorachd,
Sìor fo ignean nam Mandinka.
Mise, cuideachd, ar-a-mach
Is fàth dòirteadh fala Bengali.

Riochdaich mo shìol dubh combrùghadh
Air sgàth taisbeanadh beartais ghallt'
Is mise an cuan is na sgòthan
A shiubhladh da Gama fo sheòl.

GENIZA

Far above the smoke
And ashes, they lay
Untouched
By the breeze or
The hand of man.

Three thousand secrets;
Recipes,
Shopping lists,
School-books,
Sacred texts
Essays of philosophy …

Each one clustered,
Confused collectively,
Clasped in the attic
And ripe
In the womb of the geniza.

They maintained voices and
Memories of their nation,
Spanning a millennium's continuum
In repose, through conflict
Through unease
They would not yield their sanctuary.

Not a singular page
Would be devastated
By fire or blade;
Better to wither away.
For each Hebrew character
Contained the sacred name.

הזינגה

Fada os cionn na smùide,
Na luaithre; laigh iad
Gun ghluasad na gaoithe
No làimhseachadh duine.

Trì mìle dìomhairean;
Reasbaidhean,
Liostaichean ceannachd,
Leasanan cloinne,
Teagasg coisrigte,
Aistean feallsanachd ...

Gach uileag cruinnichte,
Na rù-rà ri chèile,
Glaste sa mhullach;
Faoisgneach
Am broinn an geniza.

Gleidheadh iad guthan
Is cuimhne an t-sluaigh,
Fad mairsinn nam mìle bliadhna.
Nan suain, tron spàirn
Tron treagamh;
Cha ghèilleadh an tèarmann.

Cha ghabhadh aon dhuilleag
A sgrathadh
Le teine no sgian;
B' fheàrr an crìonadh.
Oir eadar gach samhla Eabhrach
Chumadh comharra Dhè.

Richie McCaffery

VINTAGE CLOTHES-SHOP

The fun is in guessing where the holes come from;
moths, cigarettes or even something ballistic.

The stains on old linen too, mysterious as lichens
blooming on walls of forgotten territories.

Here, like some old shambles, the ghost of man
is butchered into its fusty cuts and sweetbreads.

I will take home something that sags hauntingly,
some wizened shoes that tell my feet where to go.

James McGonigal

WITH VACANT POSSESSION

My ears are two For Sale boards
on the conversion project of my head,

one aslant at an Irish angle to the hedge of hair,
the other more Scottish, uptight or circumspect.

This bone house features replicas, exact enough,
of every room I've ever lived in, tidied up

as if expecting viewers. I drop in frequently
to pace the floorboards or sit back

with a cup of tea. Just by itself.
The rising steam comforts my cheeks.

Why do folk call its sunset colour 'black'?

Christopher Whyte

A FACE THAT WON'T BE ETCHED ALONG
THE CREST OF THE CUILLIN

> *Die Begegnung mit dem Werk setzt jedesmal Erwartungen frei, die bei der*
> *Begegnung mit dem Autor erschüttert werden; das ist eine Grunderfahrung jeder*
> *Annäherung an die Kunst und den Künstler.*
> —HANS BERGEL

> *А кто это признал, что вы поэт? Кто причислил вас*
> *к поэтам? – Никто. А кто причислил меня*
> *к роду человеческому? – Вы учились этому? –*
> *Я не думал, что это даётся образованием. –*
> *А чем же? – Я думаю, это ... от Бога ...*
> —FROM FRIDA VIGDOROVA'S TRANSCRIPT
> OF THE TRIAL OF JOSEPH BRODSKY

> *De mondd, a tű, – az megmaradt?*
> —MIKLÓS RADNÓTI

> *Всякий триумф всегда в какой-то мере*
> *есть форма тирании.*
> —ANNELISA ALLEVA

I

When next I go north
I won't see your face
etched along the crest of those mountains.
I didn't see them
when they buried you,
my presence that day was not needed.

I won't write a lay
on the bond that links
your poetry to that part of the country,
I won't ask your fierce speech
to be heard in my verse,
or take a loan of it in my poems.

Crìsdean MacIlleBhàin

GNÙIS NACH DEALBHAICHEAR
AIR BEARRADH A' CHUILITHINN

Die Begegnung mit dem Werk setzt jedesmal Erwartungen frei, die bei der
Begegnung mit dem Autor erschüttert werden; das ist eine Grunderfahrung jeder
Annäherung an die Kunst und den Künstler.
—HANS BERGEL

А кто это признал, что вы поэт? Кто причислил вас
к поэтам? – Никто. А кто причислил меня
к роду человеческому? – Вы учились этому? –
Я не думал, что это даётся образованием. –
А чем же? – Я думаю, это … от Бога …
—BHON ÀTH-SGRÌOBHADH A RINN FRIDA VIGDOROVA
AIR DEARBHADH-CÙIRT JOSEPH BRODSKY

De mondd, a mű, – az megmaradt?
—MIKLÓS RADNÓTI

Всякий триумф всегда в какой-то мере
есть форма тирании.
—ANNELISA ALLEVA

I

Nuair a thèid mi gu tuath
chan fhaic mi ur gnùis
air a dealbhadh fad bearradh nam beann ud.
Cha robh iad 'nam shealladh
nuair a thiodhlaic iad sibh,
cha b' fheumail mo làthair-s' an uair sin.

Cha sgrìobhar leam laoidh
air a' bhann a tha ceangal
nan ceàrn ud dhen dùthaich 's ur bàrdachd,
's chan iarr mi gun nochd
àrd-ghlòir fhiadhaich ur rann
'na mo dhàn, no a gabhail an iasad.

Of those who gathered
in the mountains' gloom
there were some who kept sorrowful silence,
while others shared
diligent tales
about your awkwardness and lack of skill

in the ways of the world,
that I often heard
on the lips of those to whom your verses
were a cause of confusion
or even of shame
which they stifled as best they could.

Perhaps that was not
so different from
your opinion once you had become
honoured, venerable,
as you looked back upon
the young man you had been long ago,

severe, diligent, thrawn,
on his struggle, his love,
when you cast his poems in a new guise.
Of the verses he wrote,
you only allowed
a selection to reappear in print,

although the truth was
the years had not changed
what you believed about the deeds
of the great Stalin:
that they were not crimes
but choices born of skill and wisdom.

Measg a' chomainn a chruinnich
fo ghruamachd nan sliabh
bha cuid chuir an dòrainn 'nan tost iad,
    ach chaidh iad mun cuairt,
    na sgeulachdan èibhinn
thaobh ur mì-dhòigheileachd is cion sgil

    ann an gnìomhan an t-saoghail,
    's mi gan cluinntinn gu tric
air bilean na feadhna a b' adhbhar
iomachomhairl' i ur bàrdachd
    agus nàrachaidh dhaibh,
a b' fheudar bhith mùcht' mar a b' urrainn.

    Math dh'fhaodte nach robh
    i cho eadar-dhealaicht',
ur beachd fhèin, an dèidh dhuibh fàs
    nur bàrd urramaicht', aost',
    's sibh a' sealltainn air ais
ris an òigear a bh' annaibh aon uair,

    dìleas, dìorrasach, searbh,
    air a thrioblaid 's a ghaol,
nuair a thilg sibh dreach ùr air a dhàintean.
    Dhe na chaidh sgrìobhadh leis,
    cha do cheadaicheadh sibh
ach pàirt dheth ath-nochdadh sa chlò,

    ged nach robh e air fìor-
    atharrachadh, na bha
sibh a' creidsinn mu dheidhinn nan euchd
    rinn fear calma na stàilinn,
    nach b' eucorach iad
ach roghainn na seòltachd 's a' ghliocais.

Of those gathered at your grave,
   there were some whose mourning
was truthful and sincere; others felt
   without knowing why,
   the scene before them
was important and noble so they

   kept puffing and swelling,
   until the showers came
and they had to find themselves shelter.
   Some set down their views
   on what happened that day
in a neat, polished poem of their own,

   the ones who, perhaps, thought
   that they would inherit,
your greatness and the sheen of your name.
   Didn't they put the real
   taste of Sorley in their poems,
wouldn't they win the same fame as you,

   following you across
   inaccessible peaks?
But we must understand that they travelled
   in metaphor only,
   always comfortable, calm,
because their sort are not fond of danger.

II

I remember three occasions we met.
The last time you didn't want to say
so much as a word to me I'm sure,
your deafness was a ready-made excuse,
but the day was solemn and that did not work.

Dhe na dhlùthaich rir n-uaigh,
bha cuid ann 's an tuireadh
làn, firinneach, trom, 's cuid a dh'fhairich
gu neo-shoilleir gu robh
na bha tachairt fon sùil
allail, cudthromach, àrd, 's uime sin

bha a' sèideadh 's ag at,
gus an tàinig na frasan
is a b' fheudar dhaibh fasgadh a shireadh.
Chuir cuid sìos am barail
air gnìomhan an latha
ann an duanag shnog, shnasaicht' leò fhèin

a smaoinich, is dòcha,
gur ann aca bhiodh i,
ur n-oighreachd is boillsgeadh ur n-ainm.
Nach iadsan a chuir
fìor bhlas Shomhairle 'nan dàn
is a mhealadh an aon chliù a bh' agaibh!

Iad gur leantainn air slighe
nam bidean ro àrd
ach, feumaidh sinn tuigsinn, chan ann
ach air dòigh shamhlachail,
dòigh sìor chomhfhurtail, chiùin,
bho nach anns' leis a' chuid sin an cunnart.

II
Is cuimhne leam trì uairean a choinnich sinn.
An uair mu dheireadh cha robh sibh ag iarraidh
eadhon facal a ràdh rium, tha mi cinnteach,
's ur buidhre agaibh mar leisgeul furast',
ach bha 'n là sòlaimte, is dh'fhairtlich sin oirbh.

I stayed in my seat and held my tongue,
listening to my own words pouring from
the lips of the professor, to the speech
I'd written in your honour as he read
it out in front of the assembled crowd.

At the meal after the ceremony
the conversation between us was stumbling.
I didn't say much and the head of my
department wasn't sure what he should ask,
he'd read your work but superficially.

The second time you almost slandered me!
I gave a talk on your beloved friend,
who said a mine exploding near your feet
was not the worst thing that could have happened
to you, the poet whose wits had been

quite faltering ever since the day
of the panic in the Greek café,
with the bullets and the screams, when his
communist comrades stained the wooden floor
with blood from their wounds that was so red.

Maybe he was only there to hear
their speech, (he didn't take much interest
in the conflict of ideologies),
for the words and sayings that would come
sharp and pointed from his companions' lips.

As I spoke, I became aware of your
restlessness, you were already preparing
the bitter attack you made as soon
as I had reached the end of my oration.
What you did was rather unseemly:

Dh'fhan mi 'nam shuidhe, gun mo bhilean fhìn
a ghluasad, 'g èisteachd ri m' fhaclan a' dòrtadh
bho bhilean an àrd-ollaimh, ris an òraid
a sgrìobh mi nur n-onair, 's e ga leughadh
a-mach fa chomhair a' mhòr-chruinneachaidh.

Aig an dìnneir a lean air an deas-ghnàth,
cha robh ach tuisleach an còmhradh a bh' againn.
Cha duirt mi mòran, 's cha robh fhios aig ceann
mo roinn-sa dè bu chòir dha fheòrachadh,
bho nach deach e ro dhomhainn nur n-obair.

An dàrna h-uair, bha sibh cha mhòr gam chàineadh!
Rinn mi òraid mu ur càraid gràdhaicht',
mun fhear a thuirt nach b' e an rud bu mhiosa
a dh'fhaodadh tachairt ribh gu spreadhadh mèinn
faisg air ur casan fhèin, am bàrd a bha

a chiall-san dìreach tuiteamach an dèidh
na h-ùpraid anns a' chafaidh Ghreugach, leis
na peilearan, an sgreuchail, nuair a shalaich
a chàirdean co-mhaoineach an t-ùrlar fiodha
le fuil on leòntan, 's ise cho fìor-dhearg.

Bha e ann an sin air sgàth na cainnt
a-mhàin, is dòcha, ('s e gun ùidh glè làidir
a ghabhail ann an strì nan teagasg mòra),
air sgàth nan dòighean-labhairt, bhiodh a' tighinn
cho guineach cuimir o bhilean na cuideachd.

Fhad 's a bha mi labhairt, mhothaich mi
d' ur n-anfhois, 's sibh a' deasachadh a-cheana
na h-ionnsaigh gairg' a thug sibh orm cho luath
's a ràinig mi mo bhriathran-sa mu dheireadh.
Bha e beagan mì-chiatach, na rinn sibh:

I wasn't the only one in the hall
who felt surprise and embarrassment
along with indignation since there was
no link between your charge and what I'd said.
My regard for you was firm, established,

and I refused to answer you at all.
If that debate would not have been fitting
for your status or mine, or so I thought,
the disgrace would surely only grow
were we to quarrel with one other.

III

But why should anyone be surprised
you treated me with such hostility?

Despite all your friendship and closeness to Ireland
you were not so keen on the faith of my fathers.

I cannot be sure whether a whisper ever
reached your ears about my desire's inclination;

I do not know how you tended to look upon
those kind of questions, how severe your judgement,

but if it is true such a man wounded you
when you were young – maybe that came between us.

On top of all that you were not very friendly
with the man who taught me and nurtured my talent,

who printed the poems that came in abundance
that you never mentioned anywhere at all,

who never uttered a word in my presence
against your work's greatness, explaining with patience.

cha bu mhi an t-aon fhear anns an talla
a dh'fhairich iongnadh agus nàrachadh
a bharrachd air diomb, 's gun aon cheangal ann
eadar bhur casaid is na thubhairt mi.
'S am meas a bh' agam oirbhse stèidhicht', daingeann,

dhiùlt mi ur freagairt buileach. Mura robh
an deasbad ud a' freagairt ri ur n-inbhe,
air neo ri m' inbhe fhìn, bha mise smaointinn
nach biodh an tàmailt ach a' dol am meud
nam bitheadh sinn a' connsachadh le chèile.

III

Bha gu leòr a reusanan math' ann
sibh a bhith car nàimhdeil mu mo dheidhinn.

A dh'aindeoin ur càirdeis 's ur coibhneis ri Èirinn,
cha robh sibh ro bhàidheil a thaobh creideamh m' àraich.

Chan fhaod mi bhith cinnteach an d' ràinig riamh cagar
ur cluasan air cuspair claonadh mo mhianntan;

chan eil fhios agam mu aomadh ur barail
air ceistean dhen t-seòrsa, no air cruas ur breith;

ach mas fhìor gun d' rinn duine coltach ur leònadh
's sibh nur n-òigear, math dh'fhaodt' gum b' e cnap-starradh e.

A thuilleadh air sin, cha robh sibh glè choibhneil
ris an fhear bha gam theagasg, 's ag altram mo thàlainn,

a chlò-bhuail na ranntan bha tighinn 'nam pailteas
nach duirt sibh smid orra an àite sam bith,

nach do leig bhuaithe facal an aghaidh ur mòrachd
'na mo làthair, 's a mhìnich ur dàintean le dìcheall.

If you saw in me the godson of your enemy,
It's easy to see why my words didn't please you.

IV

But that was all yet to happen when
you and I met for the first time.

That was in Edinburgh, during the festival,
one Thursday evening, though not too late.
It was more than twenty years ago.
I cannot recall the words you used,
only how strange the situation was.

I'd spent almost ten years in Italy,
and knew just a few people in Scotland.
I was putting your work into Italian,
not just those poems that had been reprinted,
but others not translated into English,
that waited in the secrecy and strength
of the tongue in which they were put together.
There were words and phrases, idioms,
that I could not find in the dictionary.
On top of that, my Gaelic grammar
was not so strong and I needed help.

But you had no desire to explain your texts.
Instead you wanted to describe your love's misfortune:
the woman who thought up the lie that hurt you,
and the married man she deceived you with,
about whom a certain word formed on your lips,
just as my mother's lips used to form it,
as if it belonged to a savage tongue,
one spoken in a country no-one recognised,
a word I knew, as it pertained to me.

Mas e daltan ur nàmhaid a chunnaic sibh annam,
tuigear carson nach do chòrd m' fhaclan ribh.

IV

Ach nuair a choinnich sinn le chèil' an toiseach,
cha robh sin uil' air tachairt fhathast.

Bha siud ann an Dùn Èideann, an làithean na fèille,
feasgar Diardaoin, cha b' anmoch an uair.
Tha còrr 's fichead bliadhn' air dol seachad bhon àm.
Chan eil mi cuimhneachadh ur briathran,
ach 's cuimhne leam neònachd ar suidheachaidh.

Chuir mi seachad cha mhor deichead san Eadailt
's gun mi eòlach ach air beagan dhaoine 'n Albainn.
Bha mi cur Eadailtis air ur cuid dhàintean,
chan ann a-mhàin air na nochd a-rithist sa chlò,
ach air dàintean nach robh tionndadh Beurla orra,
's iad ri dàil an diamhaireachd 's an neart
na cànain far an deach an cur ri chèile.
Bha faclan ann, is dòighean-labhairt
nach b' urrainn dhomhs' an lorg anns an fhaclair.
A bharrachd air sin, cha robh mi cho làidir
ann an gràmar na Gàidhlig, 's mi feumail air cobhair.

Ach cha robh sibh idir airson ur teacsan a mhìneachadh.
Is e na bha 'na rùn agaibh neo-shealbhachd ur gaoil aithris,
bruidhinn mun bhoireannach a dh'innlich breug ur leònaidh,
mun fhear eil' leis an d' mheall i thu, fear-pòsda, 's sibh
          a' cleachdadh
mu dheidhinn facal àraidh chaidh chruthachadh air ur bilean
dìreach mar a chruthaich bilean mo mhàthar e,
mar gu robh e buntainn ri cànain allmharaich,
cànain nach robh ga bruidhinn an tìr a dh'aithnich duine,
facal a bha mi eòlach air, bhon a bhuin e rium fhìn.

I understood I had been told a secret,
and it was important for that to be clear,
but at the same time I understood you'd told
many people in different places
(two things that don't go easily together),
you loved to tell the tale, renew the intensity,
revisit all that old perplexity.

The most comical thing about our conversation,
was that we were at cross-purposes,
I had no interest in the situation
that compelled you to write the poems, the troubles
in your heart and spirit long ago,
but in the texts, and in translating them
faithfully and conscientiously.

I didn't get what I was looking for,
and got something I wasn't looking for.

I had to wait until your rival gave
a precise explanation of your poems' difficult passages.
I went back to Italy with my notes full
of grammar and language, without writing
down a word of the story you'd told me.

V

Who will anoint me?

I got no trace of oil from your hands,
no cross upon my lips, anointing my
forehead, or my arrogant cheek. You could
say, however, that if I ever had,
you'd been so liberal with it in the years
before you died that it would not have been
of much value.

Thuig mi gun deach rùn-dìomhair innse dhomh
's gu robh e cudthromach sin a bhith soilleir,
ach thuig mi aig an aon àm gu robh sibh air innse
do mhòran dhaoine ann an diofar àiteachan
(dà rud nach tèid gu furasta le chèile),
gur caomh leibh innse 's an dèinead ùrachadh,
a bhith 'g ath-thadhal imcheist uil' an sgeòil.

Is e a bha na b' èibhinne nar còmhradh
nach do choinnich sinn, bho nach robh ùidh agam
anns an t-suidheachadh a rinn ur spreagadh
gus na dàintean a chur ri chèile, ann
an trioblaid ur cridhe 's ur spioraid 'n ùine chèin,
ach anns na teacsan, 's an eadar-theangachadh
gu dìleas cogaiseach ri cànain eile.

Cha d' fhuair mi 'n rud a bha mi ag iarraidh,
is fhuair mi rud nach robh mi ag iarraidh.

B' fheudar dhomh feitheamh gus an tug ur nàmhaid
mìneachadh pongail dhomh air àitean doirbh ur dàintean.
Chaidh mi air ais don Eadailt le mo notaichean
air gràmar is air cànain, 's cha do sgrìobh mi
sìos càil dhen an sgeul a dh'innseadh dhomh.

V

Co leis a thèid mo ungadh?

Cha d' fhuair mi lorg air ol' or làmhan fhèin,
crois air mo bhilean, ungadh mo leth-chinn
air neo mo bhathais ladarna. Faodar
a ràdh, co-dhiù, nan robh mi air a fhaighinn,
is sibh cho strùidheil leis air fad nam bliadhna
san robh ur bàs a' dlùthachadh, nach biodh
cus luach ann.

The one you believed
to be your enemy, he was too modest,
too busy with teaching, publishing
and with his own poems to have
time left over to consider
heirs, successors, oil or ordination.

And so, because I was so sensitive,
to some extent I had the same feeling
that a scholar or a deacon has
after the ceremony he had hoped
would give him the right to graduate;
rising from the place he bent his knee,
without scroll, title or ointment on his brow,
he reflects that no human authority
at all can bestow the gift of new speech,
the gift of a golden tongue and skilled words,
that it's a fish, inhabiting the darkest
waters, hiding the golden gleam of its scales
until they are ready for the light.

He leaves the hallowed hall with steadfast steps.

VI

The verses will endure. Although they will say you
betrayed your language as you betrayed your poetry,
when you allowed pale English cribs to stand next to
each poem you published, like mould suffocating
the trunk that was strong, lithe and true, poisoning

every fruit that could have grown there in its absence.
The verses will endure. Despite the progeny,
that unpleasant brood of conceited impostors,
who'd rather your work was described and debated
by those who'd not even a word of your language,

Am fear a bha sibh creidsinn
gur e nàmhaid a bh' ann, bha e ro nàrach,
ro thrang le teagasg, clò-bhualadh is le
a dhàintean fhèin 's gum bitheadh
ùin' aige airson smaoineachadh mu dheidhinn
oighreachd, ola air neo sagartachd.

Uime sin, is mis' cho fìnealta,
bha 'm faireachdainn agam, gu ìre bhig,
a bhios aig sgoilear air neo deucon, is
an deas-ghnàth crìochnaichte, san robh dùil aig'
dligh' fhaighinn airson ceumnachadh air adhart,
dh'èireas bhon àite far na lùb e ghlùn
gun phàipear no tiotal no ungadh air a ghruaidh,
's a smaoinicheas nach tig gibht na h-ùr-labhairt,
gibht na teangadh òir 's nam briathran sgeilbte
a-nuas bho ùghdarras daonna sam bith,
gur iasg e, dh'àiticheas na h-uisgeachan
as doirch', 's e ceiltinn boillsgeadh òir a lannan
gus am bi iad ullamh ris an leus.

Fàgaidh e 'n talla sòlaimt' le ceum seasmhach.

VI

Ach mairidh na dàintean. A dh'aindeoin na theireadh
gun d' rinn sibh ur cànan 's ur bàrdachd a bhrathadh,
's sibh ceadachadh lethbhreac glas Beurla bhith nochdadh
fa chomhair gach fear dhiubh, mar chlòimh-liath a' mùchadh
an stuic a bha làidir, seang, dìreach, a' truailleadh

gach cinneis a dh'fhaodadh bhith ann às a h-eugmhais.
Ach mairidh na dàintean. A dh'aindeoin a' chinnidh,
a' ghuir ud mhì-chiataich de mhealltairean leòmach,
a b' àill leò gun sgrìobhte 's gum bruidhinnt' mur deidhinn
le daoine nach eil facal Gàidhlig 'nan eanchainn,

who knew not your gift to the speech of your forebears,
who worked as if language were only the wrapping
they'd throw away once they got home from the market,
to enjoy the goods that were purchased so cheaply!
They were fools, but the stupidest fool was he who said

you were just as valuable a poet in English
as you were in Gaelic, or daftness of that sort,
who founded the group distinguished in diligence,
following you, as they themselves considered it,
in creating poems in the style of mirrors,

with Gaelic and English supporting each other,
like limping creatures who could not proceed surely,
one foot with no understanding of the rhythm
followed by its fellow, those poets desiring
to triumph twice over, in two tongues, the wretches!

The verses will endure, the fine, comely stanzas
you came to despise after only a short time
had gone past since you had first put them together,
after you discovered each lie your love told you;
before your hope and your confidence failed you,

fading in the Great One who'd save sick society
and break down the barriers of poverty and violence,
who could transform (wasn't that what you believed in?)
every tribulation, but then the pale light
of the truth dawned around you and left you disgusted.

The verses will endure, despite the commitment
you lacked, abandoning your art and your talent,
neglecting the yield of the gift you were given
not knowing who gave or allowed you to have it,
which smouldered like embers in a deadened fire.

gun chuimhn' air na rinn sibh de chànain ur sinnsrean,
ag obrachadh mar gum b' e pasgadh a' chànain,
a' tilleadh bhon t-siopa 's a tilgeil a' phàipeir,
gus bathar a mhealtainn a gheibht' air prìs shuaraich!
Bu bhaothairean iad, ach b' e 'm baothair bu ghloiceil'

a thuirt gum bu bhàrd sibh cho luachmhor sa Bheurla
's a bha sibh sa Ghàidhlig, no saobh-chiall den t-seòrsa,
a stèidhich an comann bu lìonmhor an dìcheall,
a' leantainn ur dòigh, mar a bha iad a' smaointinn,
a' gineamhainn dhàintean le nàdar nan sgàthan,

a' Ghàidhlig 's a' Bheurla a' toirt taic' do chèile,
'nan creutairean crùbach nach urrainn dhaibh siubhal
gu cunbhalach, aon chas gun tuigsinn an ruithim
a tha aig a cèile, 's na bàird ud ag iarraidh
bhith buadhmhor dà uair, an dà chànain, na truaghain!

Ach mairidh na dàintean, an ranntachd ro chuimir
a ghabh sibh gràin oirre gun ach beagan ùine
dol seachad bhon tràth san do chuir sibh ri chèil' i,
's sibh nochdadh gach brèige a dh'innis ur gaol dhuibh;
an dòchas a bh' agaibh a' fàilligeadh, 'n earbsa

a' seargadh san t-sàr-fhear a b' urrainn dha 'n comann
tinn sòisealt', 's gach bacadh a thig oirnn o bhochdainn
's o fhòirneirt a shlànachadh, 's cruth ùr (no b' e sin
a chreid sibh) a thoirt air gach deuchainn, ach leus glas
na fìrinn a' nochdadh mun cuairt oirbh cho sgreamhail.

Ach mairidh na dàintean, a dh'aindeoin an dìlse
bhith dhith oirbh, 's sibh trèigsinn ur dreuchd is ur tàlainn,
a' dearmad gach toradh den t-sàr-ghibht a thugadh
gun fhios cò a thug no a cheadaich i dhuibhse,
's i fantainn mar ghrìosach aig tein' air a smàladh.

With one puff from your lips, poems would leap from them,
as beautiful and valuable as you'd written,
like flames that would illuminate every corner
in a room that once was dark. But your effort
was fleeting; once you became a famous poet,

for all your blowing, nothing came forth but ashes,
although you had plenty of excuses for it,
because every man has his excuse, his reason.
The verses will endure, because they are better
than yourself, so fluent and sure that you'd believe

they did not come from you, rather they came to you,
your nimble mouth was but art's chosen instrument
used by an intention you did not recognise.
Your poetry was wiser than the man who made it,
more perfect, enduring. Your verses will endure.

Translated by Niall O'Gallagher

> *Encountering the work invariably prompts expectations which are*
> *shattered when one meets the author: anyone who gets at close quarters*
> *with art and artists has this basic experience.*
> —HANS BERGEL

> *But who recognised you as a poet? Who told you you could be one? –*
> *Nobody. Who told me I could be a human being? – Did you take a course?*
> *– I didn't think it was something you studied. – Then how? – I thought it*
> *came … from God …*
> —JOSEPH BRODSKY

> *But tell me, the work – did it survive?*
> —MIKLÓS RADNÓTI

> *All triumphs are invariably, to a greater or lesser extent, a species of tyranny.*
> —ANNELISA ALLEVA

Ach sèideadh bhith tighinn bhor bilean, bhiodh bàrdachd
cho àlainn 's cho luachmhor 's a rinneadh leibh roimhe
a' leum aist', mar lasraichean dhèanadh gach oisinn
dhen t-seòmar a shoillseachadh. Cha robh an oidhirp
ach diombuan, 's an dèidh dhuibh bhith fàs nur bàrd ainmeil,

ge làidir an sèideadh, chan fhaight' ann ach smùrach,
is uiread de leisgeulan agaibh, oir bithidh
a leisgeul math fhèin aig gach duine, 's a reusan.
Ach mairidh na dàintean, a chionn gura h-fhèarr iad
na sibh fhèin, cho fileanta buadhach 's gun creidear

nach tàinig iad bhuaibh, ach b' ann thugaibh a thàinig,
's nach robh ann ur beul clis ach ionnsramaid ealant'
a chleachd is a dh'ùisnich rùn eile nach b' eòl dhuibh.
Bu ghlic' ur cuid bàrdachd na 'n duine a sgrìobh i,
nas coilionta, maireannaich'. Mairidh ur dàintean.

Nuair a nochdas sinn an obair, bidh dùilean air an dùsgadh annainn a thèid a
bhriseadh nuair a choinnicheas sinn ris an ùghdar. Bidh gach neach a
dhlùthaicheas ris an ealain is an luchd-ealain ag aithneachadh na bun-firinn seo.
—HANS BERGEL

Ach cò bha gad aithneachadh mar bhàrd? Cò cheadaich sin riut? – Cha do
cheadaich neach sam bith. Cò cheadaich rium a bhith 'nam dhuine? – An d' rinn
thu cùrsa? – Cha robh mi creidsinn gun deach sin ionnsachadh. – Mura tèid, dè
an dòigh? – Bha mi creidsinn gun tig sin ... bho Dhia ...
—JOSEPH BRODSKY

Ach innsibh dhomh, an obair, an do mhair i?
—MIKLÓS RADNÓTI

Bidh gach buaidh an còmhnaidh, ann an dòigh air choreigin, 'na seòrsa aintighearnais.
—ANNELISA ALLEVA

Martin MacInnes

AMERICA

The journeys are long with little in common except your blood.

The thing with my brothers was that we rarely talked and then only really about the football; it was not as if I could just carry on and broach the possibility of being dead. There was never really the right time. I think it's amazing that they were with me, while I was drowning. I'm glad that they were there, to spend that time with me, time that felt like weeks and weeks, months, a lifetime.

It was a part of the country we had never been to before. A tiny leg of land on the south-west main, a peninsula attached by a loosening membrane to the rest of the body; an almost-island.

There are no islands out here, you know, I said, attempting grandeur; open sea all the way to America. You can swim there Peter, nothing in your way.

I'd need my pit-stops. What is it, five thousand miles or more?

I want to swim, I said.

You can't swim, look at it, Peter said, it is all just rock, seaweed, and shallow water here. There is nothing to swim in.

But I had wanted to swim. We had arrived at the hotel in rain and fog, and the tiredness of our bodies left us with little to say to each other. Maybe a swim would change all that. It is a way to transform your experience of the day, I had thought; removing your clothes and entering the water, just like that, with no-one there to stop you. A magic trick.

We hadn't seen each other in several years. A reunion, three brothers. Walking over stones and getting soaked, wondering how we would fill the stretch of time ahead. A task. And the familiar disappointments of arrival. Fatigue, weariness, the dull effort in calling up statements, sentiments.

I let them pass. When they had got beyond the bank of rocks, out of sight, I made a small pile of my clothes, a dark cairn, and went into the stinging cold water, my feet rubbing onto ribbons of black seaweed, which stank of strong cheese, and had myself fall forwards, slapping onto the shallow water, pushing out meekly, flapping like a dog in a pond. And that is when I died.

On the land, my shocked body called up clouds of heat. What is that smell, Steven asked.

It's awful. Really awful.

You are stinking of what's under.

What are you doing going into the small pools, carting up weed with you?!

All that black stuff.

You will have to scrub off that stench for dinner. Take the weed from off your hair.

And one of us to share with him for the night.

We'll take the nights in turn.

The weather changed. We had been dizzied on scoops of early whisky from the black tanks in the distillery, gasoline tipped down our throats. The American women in the group turning away from just the smell as the husbands leant in and burned the tips from off their eyes.

All that outdoor light made us dream of shadows and places to lie in. Rugs and endless Sunday afternoons. Coffee and a fried breakfast, the face doused, and back to the hire-car, a mysterious contraption that we were to pilot somewhere, we gathered.

Look, what are those things on the beach?

Slugs.

Slugs? At that size? How close do you think it is? No, look, they'd be eight foot long.

They look like slugs.

Slipping out the water with ease and silence.

They are seals, you fools. Aren't they beautiful? Let's go in; perfect day for it.

Steven, from the start, had spent the most time apparently alone. I used to wonder what went on in there, unobserved. He would watch afternoon television in one of the rooms. No-one else around. But he would also wait at the windows. Sitting in the conservatory facing the sea.

You can see things, he said. They don't have skin.

What?

Under the waves.

The water retracted, exposing a white cloudy mass.

Those will be the sheep, he said. The barman told me. They live on weed. They wait huddled for the waves to break over them, take their fill, and then run together up the shore. I saw you, he said.

What?

The first day. You frightened me, walking so quietly from the water.

*

The hotel – a small place, two levels, 'boutique' the brochure called it –
seemed to be dwindling, to the point where I can't remember any other
guests in the dining room and bar. Though we had come in summer, and
though breaks in the day gave conditions fine for swimming, I remember
storms that broke the light in the hotel, so that, for the brief hours of real
darkness, we had had to use torches and candles to see. It reminded me,
at least, of times spent in the island in our youth – to the north of here
and further west – in austere homes of old old stone and hard high beds
the three of us would clamber into, helping one another up, of paintings
and the audible passing of time. Silence, wellington boots, fish, fire against
our faces in the front room, a language none of us could understand,
endless days, the clock a joke.

It didn't occur to me until later that I was already dead. Not doomed,
not fated; nothing like that. I mean dead; I had died. Something must have
happened in the rocks, slipping perhaps on the weed, which was long and
tough like linguini. Hit my head, drowned – the brothers off further along
the coast, seeing nor hearing none of it.

I guessed I'd been pronounced dead at the scene, on the shore, that I
was sealed in a bag, brought to the nearest morgue, two hours' drive. And
that it was reported by the attendant staff during the evening that I moved,
displayed 'signs of life' – I doubt it was as dramatic as sitting up – but that
the experts were unable, finally, to revive me, and that still I was watched,
for quite an unusual length of time, before finally they were sure that I
was gone, and they disposed of me.

I'm going on until I stop, until all this stops, which will suddenly
just happen. The dead know what they are doing; there's nothing to be
afraid of here.

But still it goes on. It happens, a self-continuing scenario. We all acted
as we might have done, I guess. No stranger really, at first, than the common
living days that I remember.

*

A rhythmic sound coming from round the corner of the lounge – clip,
twist, fall, repeated. Like peeling vegetables, discarding the skin.

I turned the corner, and the boy didn't stop. He was perhaps seven years
old, jet black hair, folded into his task. With his right hand he held a gutting
knife, and with his left he splayed the toes of his feet, which were raised
onto the edge of one of the tables. He seemed interested in his task, I don't
think he even saw me. There were plates of hard skin between his toes,

which he cut into, carving the feet into shape. The tough skin he cut away he then threw into the fire, where it folded and withdrew to nothing. He repeatedly cut into it, with no signs of distress. And no blood. Rather a clear thick fluid, oily, dripping down from his feet.

His hands were rough and imperfect, having just carved themselves free of a block of skin. What embryos do.

Boys, I said upstairs, we will not be eating in the lounge this evening.

There was no communication in the hotel. As I said, we never saw the other guests, and the staff only seemed to appear at meal times. The boy was different; I don't know who he was with. The phones were down; we had lost our electricity, and had no signal of our own. I hadn't noticed it at the time, but cars had stopped passing, and I don't remember the presence of our own vehicle past the first couple of days. The situation was not something I wanted to get out of; I can't speak for the others. I wasn't looking at getting away.

I thought of the morgue attendants who had seen me move. If they had been able to grasp me, grasp, that is, the current that the signal indicated, and make me established and all living again, then what would I remember? Would I forget this coast?

The place began to smell of leather, as if skins were hung to dry. It was worse in our own rooms. There was a dimming, a fading of the normal strength. I went to make a cup of tea and dropped the kettle, the saucer. I would gather it all up later. I observed that my brothers were walking slowly, as if against resistance. The blankness of air was illusion, something was hiding in plain sight, but I didn't know what. When we went to the cove, early each morning, with the seals, each at a distance from the other, I knew that soon we would lose the difficulty in walking, before long we would be supple again, revived in water.

The rocks are full of translucent fish, nervous filaments, all brain, living forever and ever. You should not stand on those jellyfish, we had been warned at the start. Mysterious creatures of the sea. They see everything, they contain the whole world within their shimmering fibre. To them, a human stands and falls in seconds. They lived with the ancients. They are open, skinless, hurting as the very first life.

They reminded me of eyes. I cannot close my eyes. I only drape them with skin. I only stare into the purple wash of skin that has not seen real light. I cannot see the other parts of what's inside me. And I cannot sleep.

*

I swear I've seen that boy before. I thought of him hacking off the excess
parts of his hands and feet; it was difficult to live on the land, difficult
for everyone.

Give me my clothes, he said.

What clothes.

My skin.

*

Still we retired to the hotel each night, my brothers and I, to its comforts,
the ease of its familiar routine, its silences and lack of questions. I think
we were afraid of the alternative, the sea, and what we might find there.
How we might live there, in its distances. What might be expected of us.
And yet the boy walked right on in.

I wondered what it would feel like, to have my skin come right off.
Would I *feel* the neutrality of being without sensation? Would I be small,
or would I be everything?

You could see the boy with the black hair step into the water until he
disappeared, and he wouldn't come back for days.

In those repetitive hotel nights I was given to thinking that with an effort
of will I could determine myself into a living creature. Sit up with a start,
raise my head above the wet weed and shadows, and throw off all this
vagueness. Day after day ebbed away, all that time with nothing done. My
brothers, myself, in the conservatory, watching the grey-cloud of the
Atlantic, tucking into breakfast, the sounds of the plate, the comments on
the food, the flat, unregarded neutrality of our last actions. I wondered if
they were embarrassed that I had died.

The more whisky we took we talked, but we talked about nothing. I think
now there was the feeling of having temporarily forgotten the most obvious
thing in the world, smiling absently, covering over how easily it had
happened, how easily the thing had been forgotten, and counting with
forced amusement on the thing coming back now any second. The days
and nights passed. Quite visibly, we were fading. Our rooms smelled of
salt, and every morning there were pools of water at the foot of our beds,
with damp prints leading away. We shrugged, said only indistinct things,
went down to the same fried breakfast in the conservatory.

This all had to draw to a close at some point, though I couldn't really
imagine how it would happen. I never could conceive of endings, of

self-ending, of feeling not-feeling. I would like to say something dramatic, the three of us perhaps lining up on the shore, losing ourselves together, becoming something else. But that's not the kind of thing we would do, really. It's not in our nature. Here we are taking breakfast in the conservatory, it is overcast, how long have we been here? Feels like we've only just arrived.

Mary McIntosh

MITHER'S ROOM

Haunds fauded intae quait,
she taks tent
as the toum meenits
pass the nicht by.

Morning smools in
on the back o the sun,
deid-lichts the spreckle
on the waa
whaur she'd killed a moch.

Pirnie-taed shune lie aneth
a crumple o claes,
taiglet wi lavender
dachlin in smaa neuks.

Hugh McMillan

HUGELSHOFER, JACKSON, GILRUTH, CHINNOCK AND BAIN

A black and white photograph:
It would be a brave colour
that would infiltrate this group,
sat gowned and booted
outside the school in 1913.
They stare at the camera
their mortar boards in unbroken line.
I see it's sunny, from shadow
and the light like a mortar bomb
bursting through trees behind,
perhaps the end of summer term.
Chinnock is the headmaster
by virtue of his moustache which is bigger
than the sum of the square
of the other two moustaches.
It is a comical moustache though you sense
you would not say this near Chinnock.
Bain does not have a moustache,
she is a woman, and has caused
a small seismic stir in the seating.
Jackson to her left
has pulled some distance away
back towards the Palaeozoic era
when women knew they were fish.
Gilruth is the joker of the group,
hat askew, he wears a quizzical look.
His hand is on a chain that dangles
from the deep folds of his jacket.
Perhaps he is thinking if he pulls it,
Chinnock will be ejected into the undergrowth,
then he could sit at last beside Bain,
remove the flowerpot from her head,
and declare his love.

Hugelshofer. Not even port
in the Headmaster's study
will cheer him up this year.
He knows the strapping lads
he coached this morning in Catullus
are marked for death.

Kevin MacNeil

ALIENS THAT WEREN'T AND A SPACESHIP THAT WAS

They were at it again.

'I'll fucking show him. Prick.' His voice was loud, snarling. 'Fucking piece of shit. I'll fucking kill him.'

I shook my head, frazzled. My wife and I had come to think of them as inhuman. Not the child, obviously, but them. The couple from hell. The wife, for whom we initially felt pity and concern, was exactly like him: screaming, selfish, enraged. They smoked and drank. Drug abusers, likely. Our sympathies diminished along with our sleep.

'Fucking arseholes, the lot of them,' he bellowed.

The wall between us and them vibrated.

Isabella gave a long quivering sigh, the kind you might hear from someone emerging alive from a car-crash.

'That poor, poor child.'

I knew what was coming next.

'No more putting it off. We have to report them.'

I moved closer on the couch and placed my hand on hers. 'Look, when we come back from Erisort we'll see if things have quietened down. They can't live like this all the time.'

Isabella nodded but her green eyes were dimmed with skepticism.

'It's as well we *are* going away. Much longer on three or four hours' broken sleep and I'll be clean out of my mind.'

We had moved in ten days ago, bright with the excitement of living in a new part of the city, and bone-weary from carrying boxes. When we fell into bed that first night we hugged and talked about how great it was to be living near the park and how cute the apartment was, with its old-fashioned air heating system and garish retro wallpaper. Our murmuring voices grew slow and sleepy and our breathing deepened and we spooned and sank into a contented sleep.

But. A scream soon woke us. Adrenalin thrummed in my heart. Isabella's hand clutched at my wrist. 'What – was – that?' She sat up and froze, her eyes wedged open in the half-light.

Noise. A deep rumbling. A high-pitched wail – a child, I thought. 'Fucking kill him!' An explosion. A woman's scream. 'Ya beauty, ya fucking beauty!' Raucous laughter, male and female. Another voice, shrieking over some horribly stirring music. Something about a species from another planet. What?

'It must be next door,' I said. 'They're watching a film – they sound drunk.'
'For god's sakes. Was that a child? What time is it?'

I brought my watch up to my good eye. 'Five fifty. Unbelievable. Just how thin are these walls?' I raised myself to a sitting position.

'They told us this was a nice area. Quiet. Why are they drunk, watching a film, when there's a child in the house?'

Racket or not, I could hear, just, tears in Isabella's voice. My heart thudded. 'It'll be okay. Must be an occasion, a birthday or something. Try and get back to sleep. We'll go and see the deer in the park tomorrow.'

'Today.'

And that – an everynight, not a one-off, occurrence – was our introduction to the neighbours from hell. Living by whatever their instincts demanded, going through life as though the only point were to be as selfish as possible. It was as if they didn't own a clock and had never spent time in civilised human society. So I started calling them the Aliens, trying to make a joke out of it, to soothe Isabella's nerves. 'They've actually only ever had one drink,' I told her. 'When they first came to Earth.' I smiled, warming to it. 'Yeah, they saw how drunk people in England get, tried out a beer, and because their bodies aren't designed for it, they've been pissed and regretting it ever since. It's one of the reasons they're angry.'

Isabella giggled. I am never happier in this life than when she laughs.

'No, yeah,' I continued, 'they were pissed at first, y'know, for months, on that one beer, but now they're sobering up, the hangover's kicking in.'

'Dear god,' said Isabella, 'how long is that going to last, then?'

Over the next few days, Isabella and I argued about alerting the authorities – and debated it, I'm happy to say, in a calm and reasoned manner. Eventually we reached a compromise. I'd been asked to read at a book festival that was taking place in Erisort, Scotland, three weeks after we moved house. I'm fond of Erisort as that's where I first met Isabella. This would be my fourth visit to the festival. If the Aliens were still causing problems when we got back, I promised, we'd contact social services.

I hadn't fully figured out my reluctance, but it had something to do with not wanting to be a snitch. What could I tell the authorities? Please lock up this child's parents because they're noisy and they drink and stay up late? Christ, my own parents did that.

We survived these first days by learning strategies. We timed our work for the mornings, which the Aliens and their baby slept through. I said to Isabella, 'The Alien suckling's temporal biomechanism has autochronously adapted to primarily nocturnal activity.'

Isabella, however, was laughing at my alien jokes less often and I had to concede the witticisms were losing their sheen, despite my comedy motto ('Repeat until funny').

My nickname for the noisy neighbours soon grew more apposite. On our fourth night in the new flat a torrent of prejudice erupted beerily next door.

'Fucking send them home if they don't like it here.'

I turned to Isabella. 'Now there's irony for you.' Her smile was so very cute, a little part of me swooned and melted inside.

Mrs Alien barked, 'Fucking stealing jobs from the fucking locals.'

'I ask you,' I said in mock horror. 'But hey – you gotta admit, they're really picking up on local culture.' This city had treated me to its share of abuse.

But Isabella was massaging her forehead. 'Dear god, make it stop.'

'I'll put the TV on,' I said, picking up the remote. 'And if it's so loud he has to come and complain, good. We'll see if the lizard tail is visible when you look closely.' I switched the TV on. 'Or the circuitry beneath the hairline.'

I paid no attention to what was on TV, it was just an aural shield. But at some point, maybe half an hour later, it was as though the volume on the TV doubled.

'What?' said Isabella, frowning. I picked up the remote and squinted at it. 'Maybe I was sitting on it.' I started pressing the 'volume down' button, glancing at the screen as I did so. A spaceship was taking off from a red planet. The spacecraft looked like a toy, all the more so as I decreased the volume. But when I muted the volume altogether we could still hear booster rockets which, I scowled to think, would not actually be audible in the vacuum of space.

Isabella and I looked at each other as it dawned: they were watching the same film next door. Very loudly, just as they did everything else.

'Maybe it's a transmission from the home planet,' I said.

'Oh, you think the planet they come from was knocked up for a tenner in Pinewood in the nineteen fifties?'

I grinned. 'What it is, they *know* there's alien life out there but they don't know these are movies. To them, these are documentaries.'

That was how we learned they watched the sci-fi channel every night (and that there was such a thing).

Our thoughts were turning more and more to the poor child. We knew he was called Rex. 'Because,' I explained to Isabella, 'his parents, when they first landed on earth, didn't realise Rex is more of a dog than a human name nowadays.'

'No', she replied, 'it's because to them he's just a pet that can look after itself. Selfish bloody creatures.'

What did poor Rex's future hold? Lack of discipline, fierce parental anger. Feral behaviour. Skiving off school. Joining a gang. 'Petty' crime and 'casual' violence. Alcohol. Drugs. An upscaling of anti-social activity, culminating in prison time. Ignorant, child-spawning sex. Dole. More jail time. Entrapment, whether within or outside of prison. Horizons of possibility shrunk down to near negligible size. No creative life, no spiritual development. A brood of hostile, deprived, impoverished children. Stress. Alcohol and/or drug dependency. More stress. Unhappiness. Six foot under in a cheap wooden box. Reborn into the same situation, different body. My Buddhist beliefs encourage empathy and my anger turned to sympathy.

'I feel sorry for them,' I said. 'They must always have had unfulfilling lives. Think of what their childhoods were probably like.'

'That,' Isabella replied, 'is why we need to let the authorities know what's going on. Break the cycle.'

'There has to be a better way, a way towards a more lasting positive change.'

'You know, what's worse than living with that,' she said, pausing dramatically and tilting her head towards the thin wall that barely screened the chaos of noise behind it, 'is living with myself knowing I heard all that going on in there and did nothing about it.'

How tiredness impinges on the mind. My rich and colourful dreams were first drained of their colour, then they disappeared completely, as if snatches of restless sleep were not enough to merit a dream.

Rousing groggily, fog-brained and tender-headed after another night of it, I turned to find Isabella awake, staring at the ceiling, unblinking. She sighed.

'Morning, my love.' I kissed her but either because of my morning breath or because of how things were, she didn't respond. 'How are you feeling?'

'Terrible. They do the drinking, we get the hangovers.'

I grimaced. Isabella had past issues with alcohol.

'Listen,' I said. 'This here is suffering. As the Buddha said – all of life is suffering. This is a – a sore reminder of that. It could be good for us. There is no I. Just as there's no self in the dreaming, there's no self in the waking.'

She turned her back on me as she sat up and searched for her slippers, 'But this is inhumane.' Her tone was cold.

'Baby, we'll meditate this through, I promise.'

'Will we.'

I spent the rest of that morning sitting in the lotus position in front of a blank wall.

Isabella did not offer me coffee or lunch, nor did she come and ask if I was going to make myself something, look at the time. So it was midday and my stomach was growling but instead of going to the kitchen, I went and sat beside her on the couch and gave her a big hug, which she received but did not particularly return.

'We'll get through this,' I whispered in her ear.

She stiffened. 'That's a fallacy,' she said sarcastically, 'There is no "we".'

In the afternoon I sat in a local café which had nothing local about it, sipping a lukewarm vanilla latte and taking absent-minded bites at an overpriced cinnamon bun. A tired jumble of mental images kaleidoscoped around my head: pictures of a grizzled man and a sourfaced woman hurling cigarettes and beercans at each other with their tentacles while a baby in a filthy cot screamed and writhed; my wife sobbing her rage into a damp pillow; a spaceship descending ominously to earth from a cold and suddenly alien sky.

I remembered my mindfulness practice and silently counted my out-breaths for a few minutes and thus gathered myself back into the moment.

The café was quiet and even had something of a relaxed atmosphere. People talked in gentle voices and listened to each other. They smiled easily and sipped at steaming drinks. At one nearby table a woman with a superior facelift was saying to a well turned-out, glossy-haired boy of about four, 'There's strawberry tarts and cinnamon buns and vanilla slices. Which one is your favourite?'

And the little boy gave a small radiant smile and clapped his hands and said: 'Any.'

Just so, he broke my heart and made up my mind.

'The sun shines constantly,' I remarked to Isabella that evening. 'If there are clouds that prevent us from seeing it, that makes no difference to the sun, which shines on. It is in its nature to do so. Does the sun vanish out of existence at night? No. In the act of being a sun, the sun expresses and fulfils its true nature.'

Isabella stared at me in shocked disbelief.

'What's wrong?' I asked.

Her tone was controlled and venomous. 'Does this sermon have a purpose?' She had never spoken to me quite like this.

'Baby, think about it with me. We're the obstacles here. The family next door are just expressing their nature their way. He doesn't know better than to yell and shout, just as the baby can't help crying.'

She folded her arms across her chest, pressed her lips together. 'That's it? That's the best you can come up with?'

'I promise you, I could go and sit down and talk to him, to both of them, for hours. And they might listen and they might even quieten down for a few days. But soon enough, the yelling and arguing and all the rest of it would start up again, that's for sure.'

'Your big idea is just to do nothing? Let them win, trample all over our sleep? Cos we're special. We don't need sleep.' Her voice was rising.

'This bitter attitude really doesn't suit you.'

'Waking up tireder than when I went to bed doesn't suit me. Being a doormat doesn't suit me. Moving to a home worse than the last one doesn't suit me. Why can't you be assertive about this? I've given you days to come up with what's obvious to anyone else. And you have the audacity to solve it with: "Let's do nothing. The problem will go away." No, you've done better than that – "We're the fucking problem!"' Isabella was shouting now.

'We prove by example.' My own voice was rising in conviction and volume. 'We redouble our own efforts at meditation and being mindful. They'll see our way of life is better. They'll want what we have. This is real. Grassroots. Buddhism. We'll show them the Way.'

She screamed. 'Aaaaaaaaaaaaaaaaaahh!' It was an animalistic sound, pure frustration, and it went on for ten or fifteen seconds

And there was a moment of grace, of silence, actual silence, and now it was broken by the sound of the baby next door letting out a piercing wail and in a second there was a deliberate hammering sound as if a fist were – in fact a fist was – beating on the wall. Thump. Thump. Thump.

A harsh familiar voice thundered, 'Quiet in there, we've a fucking baby trying to sleep here.'

And that's when it happened. Rage – utter rage – seized hold of me and shook me bodily. My arms and legs were physically trembling, all of me was, and just as I couldn't stop my body shaking neither could I control what I did next. The powerful fury marched me out our front door and across the brief corridor to the Aliens' flat and I was striking at the old wooden door again and again and again with a strength I didn't recognise. Each blow that landed on the door set it vibrating in its frame, but my hand felt nothing. I believed I could tear the door out of its hinges, if that's what it took.

Isabella was pulling at me from behind, stretching my merino jumper and trying to put her hand in my left hand. 'What are you doing? Stop it. Come inside.' Her voice was a pained whisper. I turned to her and growled. 'Get. Inside. I'm sorting this. You wanted it sorted. GO!' As I shouted the last word, she cowered back into our doorway, though I could see from her eyes that what scared her was not me, but – I turned to see what.

He was a squat man with tattoos on his neck, old faded blue-ish tattoos that were smudgy yet spoke clearly of violence, contempt, prison. He wore a dirty vest and either the flat emanated a bitter, smoky smell or he brought it with him. I idly wondered what crack smells like when he spoke out, rough and loud, from a place of withering malevolence.

'The fuck d'you want, prick?'

My fury withered.

He took a step closer. Reeked of beer and vodka. 'I said, who are you and what the fuck d'you want, ponce?'

Focus on the breath. I let out a long, slow exhalation and said, 'I'm here for you. I'll explain—'

'You what?' As he spoke, a strange little yelp of laughter seemed simultaneously to burst from him. Behind me, I heard Isabella's voice – illegible, but it was her telephone voice.

'Yes. With compassion and wisdom, we can get you out of the animal realm,' I heard myself saying, 'and back into the human.'

He shook his head as though I had morphed into some manner of creature he had never seen before.

'See,' I said, raising a conciliatory hand, 'I shouldn't have allowed myself to succumb to the anger. I'm not going to do that. I got angry. But I've now gathered my *metta*, my loving-kindness, and I'll show you how to do that, too. It means, as I'm breathing I'm thinking "May you" – about you, this is – "May you be well, may you be happy, may you be free from suffering, may you progress". The progress I mention is advancement through the wheel of life—'

A connection, swift and sure: his fist launching into my face like a boxing glove.

My reading went badly. I mean, I'm my own toughest critic, but still. My swollen face and weepy half-shut eye (thank goodness it was my bad eye) elicited sympathetic winces from the scattered Erisort audience when I first took to the stage, but the reading, as became increasingly clear to me and to the politely grimacing book-lovers, was haphazard at best. As if my mind were elsewhere – which it was; my thoughts were down South at my in-laws', where Isabella was spending a few days mulling things over.

In the hospital I'd begged and pleaded with her. There were tears, outbursts. I tried to fix things, but Isabella felt she had seen a version of me that changed her whole conception of who I am.

'I don't know who you are anymore.'

'I'm no one. There is no I. And I love you so very, very much,' I told her. 'Do you still love me?'

She didn't answer and later that day she phoned social services to report suspected maltreatment of an infant and she moved back to her parents' upper middle class home 'for some well-deserved thinking space'.

I travelled to Scotland on my own. And here I was sitting on a slab of rock at Erisort shore in the evening chill. On a croft behind me some sheep bleated their version of chit-chat at each other. To my right a rowing boat tugged at its mooring, sending ripples through the reflected stars. Overhead, I saw a star winking and – it seemed – moving. A shooting star!

No. Too slow. It was large and bright and twinkling – and had definitely moved. Of course; I recalled a news item on the hotel TV – the International Space Station was visible for a few nights. And there it was – amazing – tinily winking and flashing in the vast shimmering sky. There were human beings up there inside that flickering light right now, living and working.

I sat back on the slab of stone and looked up. The evening seemed to blacken, the bright glittering lights in the sky intensified. A seagull wheeled overhead, cold-eyed, hungry, and swooped enormously below the space station. It gave a mewling, yearning call.

A thought struck me: if all is one or if we have a creator, then all that is earthly is first of all unearthly.

The sea gestured and sighed, steadily churning its fishes and corpses alike. I leaned forward and cradled my face in my hands. My cheeks were wet with brine. As if sick of how things are, the sea repeatedly pushed itself away from itself and lunged forward in ever more desperate waves that swam up and fizzed and dribbled and hissed and fizzled out on the black wet shingle, dying flatly in gone bubbles.

I have never been myself.

Robin Fulton Macpherson

CLOSING IN

The smell of meths then of paraffin –
that's the Tilley pumped up and hissing.

The bad eternity being shut out:
black trees, black branches, barring me in.

That black eternity was inside
all along, a shadow in my brain

cast not by light but by lack of light
an original wisp of darkness.

At this other end of life, darkness
welcome when found lets starlight reach earth.

LIKE LIGHT

The chronology of gravestones, not
to be trusted.
Chipped in granite so that great-grandsons
for example
can't rearrange how the dead once lived.
But if the dead
shuffle around still, leaving Caithness
for a few days
of 'for ever' back in Sutherland
or vice versa,
we can't notice, can't tell them to stop.
Not to worry
they might say, if they could say, if asked,
if we could ask.
They might tell us our own chipped numbers
will be like light
from little waves on a summer loch.

Gillian Mayes

TELL ME THE PRICE OF A DOLLAR

There are eight lifejackets and seventeen people. Unremarkable in Indochina.

Sara and Andy take seats near the prow. Andy checks his wife's lifejacket before seeing to his own.

'We haven't done much boating recently, not since …' he's explaining to those nearby.

'Not since his by-pass,' says Sara. 'We used to go down the coast every weekend but we've sold the boat and are thinking about a cottage now.'

She's a still pretty woman who's fond of pink fleeces. Andy now turns to Wendy on the other side.

'Come on Wendy girl. Get strapped up.'

'I'm too fat for it.'

Wendy is big but in the way of a large child rather than a fat woman.

'Nonsense. Here.'

He pulls at the straps.

'There,' he says. 'An eighteen-inch waist.'

I wonder who would be last in the rush for lifejackets? Who would be left floundering in this brown and silted lake? On its edges, beachcombers are sifting for the water's castoffs. A country where everything has nine lives, except people.

'Hello! Excuse me!'

The guide calls out to Sara and Andy who have stood up to get shots of fishermen casting their triangular nets. They're always lovey-dovey in public, this pair, but in the hotel I'm through the wall from them and I'm not so sure.

'The driver says, please you sit down. He can't see where we're going,' the guide explains.

'Sorry, sorry,' says Andy.

He sits down at the front and moves a bag to let Sara in beside him. The rest of us shuffle backwards.

Tonle Sap, the lake we're on, is the largest freshwater lake in Southeast Asia and is one of the world's richest sources of freshwater fish. That's what it says in my book. The fish must be very brown, I think, but if you're hungry the colour won't matter. The tour company's booklet tells us that the lake is home to 'a very different lifestyle which can be perfectly observed from the deck of our comfortable boat. Our cruise ship visits floating villages complete with schools, restaurants and even a hospital'. 'Cruise ship' is generous for a boat which holds seventeen and needs a coat of paint.

You try to pinch your eyes into seeing what the tour operator wants. If you half close them and squint, it could be a Boudin painting, luminous shapes on a grey horizon. But you can't deny the bobbing shacks on stilts, the lines of grey clothes strung across the deck to dry. You note the dog with no walks to go, little shade to hide in, its hot head resting on the boards; and when you peer deeper into the loose awnings, barefoot children throwing stones at a tin can.

Shop-boats bring water and foodstuffs to the floating hovels. But if you live on less than a dollar a day, what do you buy?

And a hospital? There's a barge with a cross painted on it. What will it have? A roll of bandage? A tin with some aspirin?

'Look,' says Wendy.

She points to her side of the boat. A small craft has edged alongside us, so close that it threatens the occupants, a woman and three children. A girl of about ten is balancing in the prow, hands stretched out to stave off a clash with our larger boat. Once stable, she leans over to beg. The woman steering the boat has a baby spread over her lap, unsupported, on its back, limbs hanging down. It's wearing a faded orange top. A boy is sitting facing the mother, a snake wound round his neck. People on the far side of our boat cross over to take photographs.

'Don't give them anything. Remember the guide said not to,' says Sara, even as Wendy is stretching to hand over a small bunch of dollars. The girl manages to snatch them and is poked by the mother to give a smile.

'Besides, they've chosen to live like that so it can't be so bad,' Andy had pointed out at dinner the night before, in response to someone's misgivings. We were in a showcase restaurant, a place which nurtured young people for a career in catering. Eight courses were served up by smiling teenagers.

'We've lost sight of what service means in our country,' someone had said.

On the boat, I'm looking in my purse for dollars too.

'We can donate to a charity when we get home,' Andy points out.

'We did that when we came back from Indonesia last year,' Sara says.

Sara the photographer; Sara the talker.

'How amazing! Isn't it amazing! Just fabulous! It reminds me of when we were in Singapore.'

Or was it South America, the Antipodes, the Arctic Ocean? Her voice would split a penguin. I swear I'll hear it forever in my head at big moments in my life, like I still hear my dead mother upbraiding me: pride feels no pain; a stitch in time ...

'Have you been to Egypt?' I ask her on the boat. The brown water reminds me of the Nile and it seems a generous question.

'No,' she says. 'But I've read a lot and I know all about it.'

She knew all about Laos, too, where we'd been the previous week. Lush strips of densely cultivated land. Everyone is poor but no one is hungry since every family has a plot. I look at an old woman with a bamboo pole across her shoulders, supporting buckets on either side, as she ploughs her way up and down rows of green beans. A child is behind her, carrying a large watering can.

'What about that road? 'Andy asked the guide. 'It looks very new.'

It skirted the perimeter of the field, close to the base of a hill.

'It's about four years old, I read,' says Sara. 'It was built to link Ban Na Ouane with Siem Reap. Ban Na Ouane is very important to the Buddhists, you know. It's one of the oldest temples but was only found in the jungle about a hundred years ago. It's the most recently restored in the region.'

'Not really,' the guide says. 'It was restored nine years ago, before the road was even built. Before that, we wouldn't have been able to visit here if it had been raining. It would be like driving through melted chocolate. The new road was made by workmen kept on after the restoration. The most recent restoration work, by the way, has been done elsewhere.'

'But it's to do with Buddhism, isn't it,' Sara asserts.

'It all has.'

'It's Chinese and UN money,' Sara explains to us.

'More from South Korea, actually, but yes, Chinese and UN and some German as well. Most of the tourists we get are from South Korea,' says the guide.

'They don't outnumber Westerners?'

'They do. Yes. Look around when we get to Wat Visoun.'

'I have another question,' she says, keeping up with him as he leads us back to the coach.

Her ankles are swollen with the heat. I look down to check my own.

*

We're in the bar, after our trip on the lake.

'I'm going to have another white wine,' says Sara.

'Push the boat out. Why not? Look what you saved in the market,' says Wendy.

The others put in their orders. Beer, mojito, gin sling …

'Are you sure about the white wine?'

Andy is having misgivings. The wine is surprisingly expensive, until you think about a country covered in paddy fields.

Sara is wearing her new pink dress. Wendy remarks on it, fingering the silk.

'You did do well, didn't you?' she says.

'I did indeed but let's get to the table. See, if you move up here,' Sara says to one of the party, 'the couples will be able to sit together.'

'These spring rolls are delicious,' Sara's saying.

'Have they got prawns in them?'

Wendy is allergic.

'I forgot. You won't be able to have them. Sorry.'

'Would you like some of my vegetarian curry?'

Andy points to the near empty dish.

'I wonder what they eat on the boats?' he goes on.

'Fish, fish, fish,' says a Chinese woman in our group.

Her English is poor so this is an easy sentence for her.

'I guess.'

'Did any of you see what happened after we drew away from that boat?' asks Sara.

'How do you mean?' asks Wendy.

'The begging one. With the snake. After our driver – are they called drivers when it's a boat – after our driver sped off?'

'There was a bit of a swell. They got rocked,' says Wendy.

'I thought so. Do you think they were all right?' Sara asks.

'How not? You don't think they capsized or anything?'

'Good God, what makes you think that?'

Sara sounds concerned.

'When we came back that way later, they were gone,' she explains.

'Well of course, gone off to another tourist boat,' suggests Andy.

'It's just that …'

Sara pauses, picks up another spring roll, dips it into the chilli sauce, and takes a bite.

'I thought I saw something in the water,' she continues.

'What, like what?' says Wendy.

'A bit of clothing.'

'What bit of clothing? I mean, there's so much rubbish in that place ...'

'It was a bit like the baby's top.'

'In what way?'

Some of the others further down the table are beginning to listen in.

'It was the same colour. That orangey ...'

Sara's voice falters.

'Was it just the top?' Wendy persists.

'We never knew whether it was a real baby anyway,' says Sara. 'We couldn't see well enough. It wasn't moving and the mother wasn't holding it properly. She wasn't holding it like a real baby. It could have been a doll.'

'She looked too old to have a baby anyway,' says Andy.

'Oh come on guys.' Wendy leans towards Sara. 'If you seriously thought it might have been a real baby in the water, why in hell didn't you say something? Why in hell didn't you get the driver to stop?'

'Don't blame Sara,' says Andy. 'You wouldn't have shouted out either, I bet. It's very difficult to make out things on that lake. It was misty and apart from that it's plain preposterous. I bet that was it, was it not? I bet it just seemed preposterous.'

The waitress comes round to remove plates.

'Would you like another drink?' she asks, taking out her notepad.

'I need another wine,' says Sara.

Andy orders a beer and the rest of the table follow suit.

'We'll light a candle in Wat Visoun,' he suggests, raising his glass.

Philip Murnin

LOVE ON THE GREEN

I knew I was right when they told me your name – your nancyboy name.
I used to wonder if parents know when they see their new baby boy what
sort of man he'll become, or fail to become. So Mother says to Father,
*darling, do you not think this one looks like such a Walter? Or even Dear,
these wrists! This one's one for me I think. We'll call him Lawrence.* Glum
father nods his assent.

Or is it this: the name shapes the man. Once christened, Walters and
Lawrences can never become engineers or policemen or footballers. No,
they must be artists and actors and poets, like you.

We were introduced at a dinner party – gay, only in the old sense.
Our eyes locked for a whole second too long and that confirmed it. You
looked down. Older than me but shyer. Our gaze snagged again and
again that evening. I brushed past you in the hall on the way to the lav.
Your right foot touched mine under the dinner table. Then you chose
me to break the wishbone of the chicken. Across the dinner table we
competed, but it didn't matter who won the wish, it would be the
same either way.

I won the wish. I put it in the pocket of my jacket. That was all that
evening. You left. Then I left with Fiona. I'd had enough, she said. A
wishbone – enough!

Weeks passed. Then months. Then one of those nights when desperation
and the drink elbowed me from bed. Glasgow Green called. Fingers of
green fog crawled out of the Clyde. It called you too that night. No moon,
no stars shone on the hour of our meeting – not unless it was somewhere
above the murk. No smell of roses for us, just the reek of meths from half-
men. Among the rhododendrons and lurkers in the shadows, we hunted
warmth. Well, more than warmth – a moment's relief.

We found it when we saw each other. We laughed, we kissed before we
spoke. I tasted the dram you'd taken for bravery. I said to you, 'Will you
save me from Glasgow Green?'

We made a heaven of your tenement flat that summer. I remember the
wide-open windows; the sun shone a dappled spotlight through the conker
tree on our indoor picnic.

We dreamed ourselves to Ancient Greece together – two warrior lovers
in the Sacred Band of Thebes. But you as a soldier! Not you, with

your spectacles and side parting and your gentleness. You'd never have frightened the Persians at all. The Sacred Band had no use for conchies. You'd have found it easier to be one of their philosophers.

No, no, I liked it better when in our dreams we beheld the Hebrides. Our own island somewhere in the gentler south, far from Presbyterian fire and brimstone. Empty Mingulay, I had in mind, abandoned by the folk especially – just for us. Our cottage nestled on the machair. You would write poetry and plant the potatoes; I would fish and cut the peat. That would be the division of our labour. For society, once a month we'd row out to dine with the lighthouse keepers – a lovely couple in their matching Aran jumpers. We could have grown old out there amongst the Gaels. Oh my potato poet, what a lovely life we'd have made together.

With my beard and my gruff voice, I considered myself more a goat-legged satyr but you made me your muse. You wrote poetry about me. When I asked to see it, you told me I wouldn't like it. I insisted of course – I needed to check. Stupidly, I imagined you'd write like Auden or Housman. But it was better than that, you wrote like you. It made me laugh to see you sitting there between the lines. Yourself, chuckling and peeking out behind each word. I was nowhere to be found, and was relieved. There was none of our love-making, only a wisp of cigarette smoke and the taste of my tobacco lips. There was the trace of me in the strawberries we ate together that lovely Monday afternoon. Although, please, it was me that washed the plates.

I don't know how they knew it, those jeering boys, that evening we sat on the grass in Kelvingrove. Those stupid boys, somehow they knew. We kept our distance from each other. Did nothing we shouldn't. Still they saw what was between us. I blamed you. You – the blatant one. Ignore them, you said. I couldn't. I stood up so they could see the man I was. I made them run. I sent them running down that hill. I didn't come back to collect you.

It makes no sense now, but then it was obvious; I ended those months with a note, shakily scribbled and pushed through the letterbox of your flat. I knew you'd be out. Such poor words I wrote for my poet and signed only with my first initial. News would arrive with you anyway through friends of friends, delivered with other trivia, recently published articles and new poems. *You hear who got engaged?* my informant would say and in your innocence you would enquire.

If there was ever a choice, but there was no choice, I chose family love.

And afterwards? My resistance lasted weeks. Then months. A year even. Then, another of those nights, I'd picked a fight with Fiona – drunk, angry, I set out for Glasgow Green. On the way back, I passed your doorstep and stopped – longing. Longing. Perhaps you had turned the hurt into poetry, I thought. Poets made use of such things. You never did.

Chris Powici

NIGHT FISHING
i.m. Les Powici

Britten's Pond, a July dusk
mayflies hazing the flat, brown water
as the day's last rooks flowed into the trees
and you threw crusts of Mother's Pride
out among the reeds where, you reckoned,
the big carp swam like slow, fat kings.

A moth-rich summer darkness came –
some mist, grass and bracken scents,
train echoes from the bridge across Salt Box Road
but all that cool, unlucky night
our hooks hung weightless, free.

I can't remember if we blamed the weather or the bait
or if we said much at all
but I can see you, Les, settled into the shadow
of that ridiculously big angler's umbrella
a mug of thermos tea cradled on your lap
while you drew calmly on a Players Number 6
as if you'd always known
it wasn't about the strike, the catch

and isn't now
talking about you, in your garden
in the April sunlight
these forty slow years later.
These other worlds.

Maggie Rabatski

SOUP

It is October
and I am making a big soup,
the one you like –
okay, the one you really, really like.

I rose early
to cook with a slow hand,
the ham stock, the herbs, the lentils,
all the bright vegetables;
Emmylou Harris and I in the blue kitchen
singing this soup
to a crescendo.

You used to say
you could smell it
soon as you stepped off the subway from work.

Could its warm breath reach you tonight?

I'll light a candle.
I'll wear the sea-green dress.

The above English translation, 'Soup', was published in Holding,
New Voices Press, 2012.

Maggie Rabatski

BROT

An geamhradh air fàire
's tha mise deanamh prais mhòr brot,
an seòrs' a chòrdas riut-sa,
an seòrs' as fheàrr leat fon ghrèin.

Dh'èirich mi tràth
is dheasaich mi le cùram,
an sùgh-hama, na leantailean, na luibhean,
gach ùr-ghlasraich dathach;
mi fhìn is Emmylou Harris
le chèile sa chidsin
a' seinn a' bhroit seo
gu àirde.

Bha uair a chanadh tu
gun robh fhàileadh gad fheitheamh
air staidhre na subway
's tu air an rathad dhachaigh
aig ceann obair do là.

Saoil am faigh a' bhlàth-anail lorg ort a-nochd.

Lasaidh mi coinneal.
Cuiridh mi orm an dreasa mhealabhaid.

THE HAY'S IN

tonight
the sun's meadowsweet breath
nuzzles the stone walls
of the barn

while the moon stares
astonished
at a naked field

Cynthia Rogerson

LUCIANA

On her sixtieth birthday, Luciana's husband did not come home with red roses. He died instead, suddenly, while on the phone to one of his plumbers. Mid-rant about grammatically incorrect invoices, he went silent, and within minutes was lifeless. In any case, it had never occurred to him to buy flowers. Meanwhile, Luciana ironed her red dress in hopes of a fancy meal out, but it was only a half hope. She ironed slowly and felt old.

After the funeral, she begged her favourite son to let her live with him. It was too lonely in her house, too full of odd noises she'd never noticed before. She wept very sweetly as she pleaded and her son could not refuse her. His wife wasn't pleased.

'But she hates me. You know that. How can I live with a woman who hates me?'

'It's true, she hates you. But then, so do I some days.'

His wife had very irritating ways. She ate with her mouth open. She often smelled slightly sour, though she bathed daily. And compared to his mother's gnocchi, her gnocchi was like wads of wet toilet paper.

'Please don't let her move into our house, it will kill us.'

'If she kills us, we'll be dead. And then we'll not mind.'

His wife held her head in her hands and wailed, to no avail. In moved Luciana, with twenty-one bags and boxes and oddly shaped little cases. Little briefcases, which contained the photograph albums of all the family funerals she'd been to. Her grandparents, her mother, her father, some aunts and uncles. Her niece who'd died from an asthma attack. Not including her own husband's funeral, oddly.

'Why do you not want a photograph album of Papa's funeral?' her son asked.

'Because he didn't love me.'

'Of course he did, Luciana,' argued her daughter-in-law, who was shocked. 'He was your husband for forty-two years.'

'We married because I was pregnant. Our parents, they made us marry. You know this! A whole lifetime paying for one mistake.'

'How can you say I'm a mistake?' cried her son. 'I'm an entire human being, you can't wish I wasn't here as if I amounted to … some milk spilled on the floor.'

'You are a better man than most, my love,' said his wife.

When she said things like that, he forgave her the toilet paper gnocchi. 'This is true,' he said. 'I might be the best man in this province.'

'Stop!' said Luciana. 'The mistake was in marrying, not in having you. You're the finest thing I ever made. Don't tell your siblings. But your father … he never loved me. You cannot fix this.'

'But all those tears!' he said.

'You are so sad without him!' insisted her daughter-in-law.

'I am not unhappy because he's dead. I'm unhappy because I was never loved by him. Now my life is over.'

'Mama! How can you talk like this?'

She sighed as if she was ninety-six. At the end of the exhalation, she said: 'It is easy to talk like this, because it's true. I'm tired of pretending otherwise. I am exhausted.'

'Are you sure you're not just a little bit drunk?' asked the daughter-in-law.

She held up the empty limoncello bottle.

'Yes, I am drunk. But it's still all true. I am a woman no man has properly loved.'

'I love you,' said her son, in a loud peevish voice. 'I am a man. And all your other sons, and my sisters' husbands, and your grandsons – all men who love you.'

The daughter-in-law counted silently on her fingers. 'Seventeen males love you.'

'You do not understand. I'm sorry, but you cannot understand. I am unloved.'

No one knew what she meant. The family decided she was insane with grief and left her alone.

One day, about a year after the funeral, Luciana was walking the family terrier when a man approached her. A small man with a big paunch – not a manly beer belly, but one that softly bunched out above and below his belt.

'Luciana? Is this you? Is it possible?'

'Yes.' She squinted at this man. Frowned. She'd been deep in her usual no-man-has-ever-loved-me sulk. 'Who are you?'

'But you have not changed at all! Still as beautiful as on your sixteenth birthday! I am Antonio of course.'

She froze, and as she stared, a much younger man emerged from the stranger's face. A handsome face, with eyes that laughed. She felt something tugging at her chest, and she smiled for the first time that year. It had been so long, her lips actually cracked, and her heart rushed blood to facial muscles that hardly knew what to do with it.

'Tonio?'

He'd never been her boyfriend, but oh how she'd wished he was. He'd been the boy all the girls in school liked, despite his shortness. From age thirteen, always a girl in love with him, and he was always sending flirty winks to Luciana as they passed in the hall. Winks which made her stomach melt, because they seemed to say:

You next, girl.

'What are you doing here? I've not seen you in ...'

'Almost fifty years, Lucici.'

The cheeky nickname he used to have for her, still fresh on his tongue.

'But why?'

'Why not? My marriage, it is over. My sister still lives here, do you not remember her? And so here I am, back home again, and who do I meet? The most beautiful girl in the school, out walking her dog.'

She quickly looked at the dog, having forgotten his existence. Yes, still at the end of his lead, thank goodness.

'Well, since you asked, I would love an espresso in your kitchen. Thank you, thank you, thank you.'

She might have invited him, she told herself as he took her arm and they walked back to her son's house. It might have been that she didn't hear her own voice. Anyway, there was a current running from his arm into her own arm, and it paralysed all thought, all speech, almost all movement. Somehow she managed to keep walking.

She made their espressos and she tried to ask him about the life he'd had, the huge clump of years of his absence, but instead he pulled her plump sixty-one year old body on to his lap and tickled her. She laughed like a little girl. She almost peed, she laughed so hard. She laughed at the picture they must make, the way they would look if anyone were to open the door right now. How ridiculous, at their age! How delicious! Oh my my!

'I love you! I love you!' they exclaimed simultaneously, then collapsed with giggles again, because that too was hilarious.

At last, here was love. The love story she had read about in a hundred novels, heard in a hundred songs. Her long marriage had just been a ... an aberration; she was obviously born to love Antonio. When he touched her, she was a girl again. Making love with Antonio was literally *making love*. Like making gnocchi out of potatoes and egg and flour. Something new existed when the process was over, though nothing new had been added. Had she felt this way in the beginning with her husband? Those distant days of fumbling and worrying if her breasts were too small. No, she had never felt this way, not even once. This was new, this was mad-making, this was the life force itself, pushing through her drab old defences. If she ever began to analyse it, all she had to do was hold his hand to feel sedated again.

The sons and the daughters were not pleased. No, no, no. Their mother, walking around with that besotted look on her face. Blushing whenever he spoke or looked at her – or worst of all, whenever he touched her.

And he touched her all the time.

He held her hand under the table, touched her knee when he thought no one was looking, put his arm around her shoulders when they sat on the sofa. It was disgusting. It made them want to vomit. Antonio came visiting every single day about ten in the morning, and did not leave until bedtime. His eyes followed Luciana around the room, and he sprang to her service whenever the least need arose. To open a cupboard door, to pull a chair out, to pour her wine. Their father had never acted like this. He'd been a distant man, a successful businessman they respected. He hadn't touched his wife like this in front of them, not even for photographs, and no one had wanted him to.

They discussed Antonio endlessly whenever he was not present, which usually meant on their mobiles during work hours.

'Where has he been all these years, that's what I want to know. I bet he's been up to no good. Why come back, if he isn't running away from something?' spat the daughter-in-law. She might feel hated by her mother-in-law, but her protectiveness was still fierce.

'He has no money. A man his age, with nothing. No land, no family aside from that sister we never see,' said a daughter.

'That's why he's after Mama, and she's so naïve, she believes he loves her. But it's only her money he's after,' said a son.

'Yes! He wants her house! Her land! Her pension!' agreed the son she lived with.

'And why did his wife divorce him? He must have done something very wicked. And his daughter, she never comes to see him. Ever,' said another son.

'Maybe he was a wife beater. Or a child molester. Or a mafia man. Or an adulterer many times over, with diseases.' A normal adulterer was not, after all, such a crime, even to these children. It was common knowledge their own father had kept a mistress.

No, no, no, Antonio was a very dangerous man, and their mother would not see it.

'Mama, we are sorry, but we don't like this Antonio. In fact, we hate him. We think he is dishonest and suspicious,' announced her favourite son, after a rare dinner without Antonio present.

'Why do you want to ruin my happiness?' Her stomach felt something hard and heavy lodge there.

'Mama, he is a con man. A charlatan.'

'He tells me I am beautiful. I know I'm not, but with him, I am.'

'You are beautiful, Mama.'

'It doesn't count when you say it.'

'Ah Mama! It was so easy for him to seduce you. Don't you see? And what does he have to offer you? He has nothing.'

'He wants to marry me.'

'If you marry him, you will lose Papa's pension. And if you die before him, he will own our house. Our own house, which sits cold and empty since you moved out. It is our house. You cannot marry him. You must not. We forbid it.'

A cold silence descended over the pasta.

'You break my heart. But I will marry him anyway. I love him.'

What did it all remind her of? Oh yes. Her parents, marching her reluctant stone-faced self up the aisle, to marry a man she did not love. All these people who loved her, telling her who to love and who not to love! It made her stubborn, realising this. It made her feel like marrying Antonio today, right now, and to hell with the family.

Antonio always had his camera with him, and he took a million photographs of the family and of Luciana.

'Quick, quick,' he would say. 'Hold still. Sit there. Smile!'

Click, click, click.

Photos of their birthday dinners, their toddlers taking first steps, of the teenage grandsons playing football, of the daughters in the kitchen, making mounds of ravioli. Hundreds of posed family photos too – they never quite had the nerve to refuse, and the sideboard became cluttered with dozens of framed family photographs. They were good pictures, despite the fact each one of the posers hated the photographer. They were, at heart, a vain family. They loved themselves! They were the Giambostianis!

When the family went on holiday and Luciana stayed behind to look after the dog, they suspected Antonio stayed overnight with their mother. When they returned, a neighbour confirmed their fears.

'His car, it is there at midnight, and still there at dawn every day.'

They were angrier than ever, and fuelled each other's hatred of Antonio. He became the devil.

'Mama, you *must* end this,' whispered her son, when Antonio left the room for a few minutes. 'He is making us all unhappy. Every time we see him, we feel ill.'

No mother can be permanently impervious to her children. Their bile began to seep into Luciana's mind. To infect her. The spell was not broken over night, but she began to see him as they saw him. Just a little at first, just a quick little splash of acid, a sudden chilling of the heart. His solicitousness began to seem a little repulsive. Why did he try so hard? His charm began to seem too oiled, too gushing. How many women before her had fallen for this greasy charm? And what about the daughter he never saw? He must have done something terrible. Now, when she took his hand, she felt nothing.

Then came the chilly November afternoon they were alone in the house.

'Luciana. Something is wrong. What is the matter?'

'Nothing.' Suddenly embarrassed by her disloyal thoughts.

'But you will not look at me.'

She turned to him.

'Lucici. Tell me what has changed. Your eyes are so different. Come here.' He patted his lap.

At first she shook her head, then she stiffly came and sat, and he put his arms around her. He was not a big man, and she was a roly poly woman, but she curled up like a little girl on her daddy's lap. Let her head drop onto his chest one last time. Now the end had come, she felt sorry for him.

'We must part, Tonio.'

'No. Please.' His voice was low, almost inaudible. She could feel it vibrate inside his chest.

'Yes we do. I'm sorry.'

'But why?'

'I don't love you anymore.'

Was it true? She felt numb, hearing her own voice say those words. He stroked her head, and was silent. For a moment, she felt her heart begin to melt again, to lurch towards him in that old mindless way. But she slipped off his lap, and he put on his coat and left. She didn't say goodbye, and neither did he. The door closed quietly. She sat at the kitchen table, and the noise of the closing door seemed to go on and on.

The winter passed, then spring, then summer and autumn. Luciana moved back into her own house and made a life by herself. The quiet grew around her like a comfortable old robe, and she was not afraid of the odd noises anymore. She was still lonely, but it was a different loneliness, with the memory of passion and romance and disillusion. Now she knew what the songs were about. She had wanted romantic love, and she had got it.

Her children were back to being relaxed around her, which mostly meant they ignored her. A relief. Was she happy? Of course not, but happiness was hardly the point, was it? She was sixty-four, and most days she was glad to be alive. If she thought of her husband now, it was always with a forgiving little sigh – loving Antonio had overlaid those other years, quelled her long resentment.

Yes, she had been unloved by her husband, but he had also been *unloved by her*. She had been a terrible wife, a passionless critical wife. And now, at least she was alive and had seven lovely children to fret over, whereas he … cold, and under the sod. Poor man. Poor lonely man, driven to a mistress for company. At last, she began to fall a little in love with him, in a maternal way. Remembered some of his kind acts; the way he kept her windscreen fluid topped up, the way he never forgot to put the toilet seat back down. He never once suggested divorce. She began to take flowers to his grave on Sundays, and light candles for him.

Antonio had been the aberration, and she thought of him rarely. Once, from a distance, she saw him in the supermarket. Just a little man with the beginnings of a stoop – what had all the fuss been about? He probably had another woman just behind him, in the condiments aisle. Some other lonely widow, ready to believe all his flattery.

Or.

Or.

Or perhaps he was alone and lonely. Perhaps he had truly loved her after all, and she had broken his heart. Perhaps her first instincts had been the right ones, and her children had been mistaken.

She had a sudden idea that Antonio's incessant photograph-taking might not have been a parasitical ploy, but the poignant strategy of an outsider who sensed he would never be invited to be photographed with them.

Into her mind came that first evening when her children had gone away, and Antonio stayed the night. How they had felt like naughty teenagers, walking naked around the house. Singing and kissing and dancing and drinking prosecco. The dog had seemed to think he was part of their relationship, and followed them from room to room, sometimes yipping from sheer joy. She had not slept a wink that first night, how could she? She hadn't wanted to miss a second. She'd watched Antonio sleep as the dawn came, and told herself she was like a woman in a romantic novel. That she was beloved.

And now, there he was, with his shopping trolley half full, looking just like any other middle-aged man. Entirely average, not an ounce of magical power in that slack face. Yet they might have married, might have been happy for a few decades. She would be helping him shop right now, smelling the melon to see if it was ripe, squeezing the bread for freshness. Nagging him to get the expensive olive oil, not be such a cheapskate, always buying the inexpensive stuff.

Imagining this, her glorified deceased husband shrivelled to nothing again, and Antonio ballooned back into the lost love of her life. She blinked hard, and wham! Her husband reverted to the real thing, centre stage, while Antonio slunk away, a fraudster in disgrace. Another heart beat, and both men became one dimensional nothing men. Strangers.

Oh! It seemed that all her life, she'd been waiting for life to make sense. A point where she could sigh contentedly, look back and see that everything fitted, because it all led to this one good certainty. It hadn't once occurred to her that life could fizzle out raggedly, with no conclusions drawn, husbands dead before they were appreciated, lovers hastily judged, jobs half-finished, dreams hanging like loose threads in a torn bit of material, too frayed to mend. Her life was winding down like a novel with the satisfactory last chapter ripped out.

*

Yes, yes, permanent truths had eluded her, damn them! But wait – hadn't there been moments of calm and clarity, of at least the illusion of certainty? For a second, she visualised all these moments, brief bursts of happiness packed down together, and it was obvious – compared to the rest of her life, they amounted to the shape and size of a medium margarita pizza. Yet a medium pizza was better than no pizza, right? Maybe a pizza was all anyone got. She sighed and turned away before Antonio spotted her. Left the store, though she had not bought her groceries.

The next day was Sunday, and Luciana was in her kitchen making gnocchi. Three of her children were coming for dinner, with their families; she'd need over two hundred gnocchi. She forced the boiled potatoes through the press, broke eggs into them, drizzled white flour with her hands, till the consistency was perfect for kneading. It felt good, the rhythmic pummelling and pulling. She imagined her family eating this, her triumphant, noisy family, enjoying it, drenching it with the creamy gorgonzola sauce she was going to make. She could visualise their satisfied mouths chewing, their throats greedily swallowing and, before the bowl was empty, their voices would offhandedly demand: Mama! We want more gnocchi!

Meanwhile, fifteen miles away, Luciana's favourite son and his wife opened a bottle of rosé. They often enjoyed this aperitif before heading to Luciana's for Sunday dinner. Football was on the television, and they both sat on the sofa watching. The children were upstairs, watching their own television. The wife suddenly said:

'You'll never guess who our new secretary is.'

He sighed. It could be very irritating, the way she talked through the game sometimes.

'The daughter of that man.'

'What man?'

'Antonio.'

'No!' He muted the sound on the television.

'Yes. I know – spooky eh? She exists! I didn't tell her who I was.'

'Good. So?'

'So, over coffee she's telling me about her father, because that's why she moved here. She says she'll never forgive herself, for abandoning him. For believing her mother's version of events. Apparently, Antonio's wife was having an affair with his boss. They said her father was a thief, that he embezzled from the company and gambled away all their savings. None of it was true, but the daughter didn't know that. He wrote to her every week for a year, then every month for three years. She never once wrote back. Now she hates herself. She says he's too honest, too gentle to live. He wouldn't hurt a fly.'

'Jesus. What does she look like? Like him?'

'A little. But in a nice way. I liked her.'

'Huh!'

'Yeah. Huh.'

Pause. He turned the volume up again and poured his wife a little more wine. He told her he would drive, if she drove home. He stared at the football game, cleared his throat and said:

'Well! No need for Mama to know this.'

'Oh absolutely. No need.'

Then they gathered their children, locked their house and drove to Luciana's house, stopping on the way to pick up some red roses. Luciana always loved flowers, and they hadn't given her any in a long time. The dog stayed behind and howled.

Andrew Sclater

THE SCOTSWOMAN WHO MARRIED INTO
THE HOME COUNTIES

Like tweed like pearls
like fire like wood
like loss like Listen with Mother with me

Like prayer like water
like a Scots laird's daughter
like your three darling war-dead before me

Like heather that shrivels in Hampshire
like silver birch going sick on the chalk
like your loch all clogged up beyond the border

Like grin and bear it
like you limp to the shop
like bravery how I wanted to shake you

Like you meant the marriage
like you could not
stop him being like he was

in his unlikeness
like a moor set down in a wheat farm
like your composure stiffening

Like your bad hip
like the smell of you ageing
like you knowing of the coming

of your death all the time he poured beer
that last evening in Broughton
like you never were like yourself down here.

Helen Sedgwick

PRECOGNITIVE ABILITIES

The cards lie face down between us on the table. It is May, and it is beautiful. I've brought flowers with me – a ribbon-tied bouquet of purple and pink – and a packet of chocolate gingers. It's the first time I've been to this suburb. The first time I've been to Zara and Ross's house. I got lost among the neat gardens and wooden fencing and dappled tree-lined streets. It's only a few miles from where I live but it feels like much further.

Zara discovered her gift when she was eight. She tells me this as she touches the cards, one by one, as if they are precious.

'The Tarot deck has seventy-eight cards,' she explains.

Twenty-two are major arcana, like The Lovers, and The Fool. The other fifty-six are minor arcana and are divided into suites of Swords, Cups, Wands and Pentacles.

Her long flower-patterned top settles over her lap and her hair is loosely pinned up on top of her head. She's not a pretty woman; a large chin protrudes from her doughy face. I can see that Ross loves her by the way he's looking at her.

She asks me if I'm doing okay. Her expression is sympathy as she speaks, and I wonder how much she knows. People talk. Especially the people at work, so Ross has probably told her what happened. I make my face look grateful so she knows I appreciate her concern.

'These things are all for the best,' I say.

She nods. 'Yes, all for the best.'

She asks me if I really believed we were going to be married and I think about the question but don't answer straight away. The truth is that I could never imagine going through with it. Instead I say:

'I was wearing the ring.'

It's Zara's turn to be quiet for a second. Then she smiles at me and says, well, one in three end in divorce these days anyway.

Ross takes her hand. 'That's true,' he says. 'One in three.'

They look at each other for a moment and I feel like I've intruded on their world, like I'm pressing in against it even though I don't belong.

Zara tells me that, in her experience, predictions of the future are accurate ninety per cent of the time. I don't know where she got that statistic from, and I don't ask. It would be rude and I think she's a nice woman so I smile and nod even as I'm thinking: ninety per cent of all statistics are made up on the spot.

'I'll make some tea before the reading,' she says.

From the choice offered I go for peppermint, even though I'd prefer a coffee.

While she's away, Ross tells me that she's given up coffee. 'That's why she only offered the tea,' he says. 'And we're trying to eat organic.'

Then he lowers his voice, as if he's about to tell me a secret, and says that he's thinking about marrying her. He doesn't want to marry her yet, but he's decided that next year he'll marry her. I know he doesn't mean it in a bad way. He's just secure in his relationship, and in the way things work. I don't think Zara knows he's planning to marry her next year. I don't know what she'd do if she did.

Mine are not the only flowers in the room; there is a bunch of white and yellow roses in a tall glass vase over by the bookshelves. The light spills in through the bay window, highlighting the photo frame on top of the old piano and trickling over the soft beige carpet. I look down at Ross's slippered feet. Maybe I should have taken my shoes off at the door.

Ross tells me that Zara's abilities have really helped him. He says that she's very good at reading the cards. 'She has a natural talent.'

He looks quite proud as he says this, as though her talent is reflected in him, and that's when he tells me that he has abilities as well. He says that his dreams come true, and I become suddenly conscious of my raised eyebrows.

He wants to explain to me how it works. He says that he'll dream something one night and then, maybe a day or so later, what he dreamed about will actually happen.

'That must be very interesting for you,' I say.

'Sometimes it's good but sometimes it's not so good ...'

I wait for him to continue.

'I mean, when I dream of bad things happening, that means I'm going to have a bad day soon.'

He laughs as he says this, and I laugh too.

'Yeah, I guess that's not so good,' I say, and I'm careful not to use words like psychosomatic, or causality.

I ask him how often his dreams come true, and he says it's not all of them – only about fifty per cent – but that he always knows which dreams are the true ones. That must be nice. Then, as if it's an explanation, he tells me that he's been reading about multiverse theory. He forgets that I used to be a scientist, or that I used to be anything other than what I am now. A lot of people do that. I don't really mind.

'I like multiverse theory, too,' I say. 'I like that there are lots of different versions, lots of different ways to imagine different universes.'

He says that he likes to think that in some universe everyone's dreams come true, because every possibility is played out.

'I'm lucky,' he says, 'because in this universe I'm the one with precognitive abilities.'

The peppermint from my tea smells sweet, and I cradle the cup in my hands when Zara passes it to me. Ross gets up and says that he's going to do some work in his study. He looks at me as he closes the door, as if I will be changed the next time he sees me.

Once he's left the room Zara begins the reading. I surprise myself by feeling nervous. The first card she turns is 'The Star.' It features:

—A naked woman pouring liquid from a jug.

—A dark pool of water.

—A sky of silver and gold.

She tells me that it's in the 'love and me' position, that it means I will come to understand who I truly am as a result of a relationship. I nod and smile, not knowing what to say to that.

'It means your feeling of being a stranger in a strange land will vanish.'

I look around, wondering if I'll be able to see it go.

That prediction is probably true of everyone, sooner or later. What would she have said if it had been a different card in the 'love and me' position? Statistically speaking, the chances are one in seventy-eight of that particular card being there. I look at the two cards either side of it. The chances of each of those cards being laid down on their own is one in seventy-eight, but the chances of all three cards being laid on the table together is one in four hundred and fifty six thousand, four hundred and fifty six. 456456. I know that because I looked up the number of cards in a Tarot pack before I came to the reading, along with my old notes about probability and statistics.

The phone starts ringing in the other room, and we both stop and wait for it to be answered before continuing. It's as though something important is happening here that can't be associated with everyday things, like phones ringing. Ross's voice doesn't carry all the way to us, but we can hear the low tones vibrating in the background as he takes the call.

The second card that Zara turns over is the eight of swords, in the 'situation' position. This time, I see:

—A woman in a long red dress, bound with rope.

—A field of daggers stretching to the horizon.

Zara says this indicates a relationship that is characterised by criticism. She says: you owe it to yourself to question how much you are willing to put up with. I think: done that. Next?

We can hear Ross walking about outside the room, up and down the hall, kitchen to study perhaps. I take another sip of my tea. The Seven of Wands is just a man in a green tunic standing on a cliff face. It is in 'challenges', and is telling me to stay focused on achieving my personal goals. God, I need a coffee.

Zara looks at me like she wants to know what I think of the reading, but instead I ask her when she's due.

'August twenty-ninth,' she says.

That's my birthday. What are the chances of that? I wonder if the pregnancy was planned, but I'm pretty sure it wasn't. When I tell her that the twenty-ninth is my birthday she asks me how old I'll be, and her lips part in surprise when I tell her I'll be forty this year.

Statistically speaking, it becomes sixty per cent harder for a woman to conceive after the age of forty. But that's irrelevant. I've never wanted children.

'What were you and Ross talking about?' she asks me, to fill the silence.

I smile and say: 'The universe.'

'Is it true, that there's a lot of empty space? A lot of voids?'

'Not necessarily.'

I take a sip of my tea and start telling Zara about dark matter. Her eyes light up when I say it – dark matter, like mysterious art, like magic, like fortune telling.

'There's a lot of space that looks empty to us, but then there must be a lot of stuff out there we can't see.'

'So what is it then?' she asks.

'We don't know.' I shrug.

I say that one interpretation of string theory is that there are many universes existing at the same time as ours, but in different dimensions. Dark matter can't be seen, or touched, but it interacts gravitationally, so although we can't see it we know that it must be there. Some people – and I'm clear that it's not part of the standard model, it's just an idea – some people think dark matter is just regular matter in another universe that's pressing against ours, and changing it. She nods as I talk, as if she believes it, as if it makes sense with the way she sees things. Perhaps people are not so very different from one another after all.

'And so, that God particle that's been on the news,' she asks me, 'what does that do?'

She means the Higgs boson, and I want to tell her that it has nothing whatsoever to do with any God. Instead, I say that it gives things mass. Finding it confirms some of the predictions in the standard model of our universe.

'Without it, we can't explain why there are stars or galaxies or anything,' I say. 'So, in a way, it makes it possible for things to exist.'

She strokes her stomach in the way that pregnant women do, and for a second I don't know where to look.

'So now we know the standard model is right, after all?' She asks.

She sounds disappointed, not amazed like she was when I talked about dark matter.

'Well, sort of. But I've always preferred the idea that the standard model might be wrong. Or, at least, up for negotiation.'

She smiles at me, and for a second she looks much younger than she is.

'There are still plenty of things we don't understand,' she says. I think she's talking about the Tarot cards, and I nearly laugh before I realize that she might mean dark matter, or string theory, or quantum physics, or the reason I came here looking for answers in the first place.

I can hear Ross moving about in the kitchen now. The smell of coffee drifts in deliciously and I imagine dunking one of those chocolate gingers in a strong cup of black, or maybe white. Everything about their home feels homely, and worthy, and so different from mine. It must be such a safe way to live; it must make things seem certain. Zara lays out more cards for me and I wait, watching the slow and deliberate movement of her hands. A part of me feels jealous.

'Do you have a particular question in mind?' she asks me.

That's a good question. It makes my head spin. I forget about science for a second, and things become personal. I wonder if I should try internet dating again. I wonder if biting my nails all the time makes me less attractive. I wonder if I should have got married.

I wonder if Zara does have the answers after all.

'Would you like milk with your coffee?' Ross calls out from the kitchen.

Even that question hangs, waiting for an answer that doesn't come.

When I look up, I realise that Zara has re-shuffled the cards.

'I'd like some too,' she calls out, 'black, with sugar,' and her face brightens up. 'Living dangerously.' Then she leans closer to me, touches my hand where it lies between us on the table and says quietly, as if it's a secret:

'Can you tell me more about those different universes of yours?'

Emma Sedlak

LET THE DAY PASS

Emptiness is a human right. Tattoo the veins
onto your arms; learn how your blood runs without you.
Board a train and stare down the world.
Set your hair alight to know that things still burn.

For a while, let part of you die. Don't apologize.
Use your soul's coffin as a soapbox
if the cat ever gives your tongue back.
Your time will come, just wait.

Meanwhile, sleep dormant under sofas
or hide, or hibernate. When friends come,
scrawl Do Not Disturb on a worried face.

Let the day pass. Know most instruments are hollow
which is how and why they sing. Don't fill the void.
Lie awake with everything and anything.

Raymond Soltysek

SONGS OF OTHER PLACES

Alice told the boys she'd make a pie. They're still young enough to like her pie, though they're growing up fast. Charlie got em a BB gun last summer, and they shoot bluejays and the songdogs that come wandering past the back fence, though they aint gonna do much harm to a songdog with a BB gun. They're asking for a .22, and Charlie says maybe next year, but she thinks the year after if that, if she can stop em hollering about it.

There's gonna be a thunderstorm for sure. The fan's rattling cause it aint keeping up with the heat. Alice wipes her brow and just knows she's left a big streak of flour across her forehead cause it feels kinda sticky. There's a line of sweat down her back and it pools at the base of her spine, and she's just waiting for that chill that'll tell her it's coming.

Alice loves thunderstorms. She watches em from the back porch, the clouds rolling over the house and the lightning snapping, and just for a moment, the trees and the back gate and the boys' swings all stand still and hold their breath and wait for the crack of doom to rain down on their heads.

She feels alive then.

Roger Hernandez died in jail last night. The State of Texas put him to death for killing that State trooper that tried to stop him the night he was smuggling his wife's cousins in from Mexico. She wrote him, just once, but Roger Hernandez said thank you, it was sweet of her to remember him, but he was a married man and he didn't wanna be taking advantage; but if it was okay with her, he'd write sometimes, tell her how he was feeling cause he didn't want to burden his wife. Alice thought that'd be okay. Made sure she wrote him from the library though, care of, didn't know how she'd explain it to Charlie otherwise. Abby, her best friend from high school, she's the librarian, said of course she could do that, and she'd keep any letters for her.

She kneads the pie dough, working through the flour, egg slipping between her fingers, strong fingers she has, and she knows how to knead dough cause her momma showed her how. Saturday afternoons, she'd park Alice up on a big kitchen stool and they'd be side by side, her momma baking big pies, apple and blueberry and pumpkin, and Alice made little pies with the same fillings that she'd feed to her dolls. Momma would sing Buddy Holly songs, sometimes whip her off that stool for a dance, whirling her around the kitchen, *Every day, it's a gettin' closer, Goin' faster than a roller coaster*, and she'd lift Alice high and they'd bump noses at the *Love like yours* bit.

During foaling, Roger Hernandez stayed in the hayloft above the barn, put up some walls with bits of lumber and bales of hay, ran a line from the generator so he could have a little hotplate and an old Dansette cassette player. Momma loaned him some Buddy Holly tapes, and he used to play mariachi bands, and Alice would sneak in and hide underneath the hayloft and listen to those horns. Then he got inta some other stuff, foreign like, first kinda Frenchy or European, then strange instruments she'd never heard before, and women's voices that seemed to fit together in ways that didn't sound quite like it shoulda. She asked him once, 'Roger Hernandez, where does that music you listen to come from?' but all he said was, 'Little Alice, they come from other places, far, far away.' They have camels there, he said, as well as horses, and the grasslands go on forever, even bigger and wider than the Prairies. 'They don't sing right,' she told him, and he said she was right, but it wasn't really singing. 'Ululating,' he said it was, and Alice reckoned the word sounded like the singing.

Momma never liked Charlie cause he didn't like Buddy Holly, said he'd be the kind of dweeb he'd have kicked shit outta at school. That was Charlie, number one jock, alpha male; heck, the first time she saw him, at that Thanksgiving dance at the Baptist Hall, she got an itch for him, just like most girls did, and he didn't dance with her all night but she was so proud when he picked her to take home that night.

'I'm gonna marry you, Alice Gantz,' he said in the car after they'd necked a while.

'Well, you oughta woo me first, Charlie Springer. Girls like to be wooed, you know.'

'No need, Alice. I'm gonna marry you.'

He did, of course. What Charlie wanted, he got. He took.

She works the dough into a ball, wraps it in plastic wrap, puts it in the refrigerator. Aint much in there; six pack of Bud, bottle of tequila, some burgers and hot dogs. She knows she don't eat right, she feels the weight gathering round her thighs and she don't like it much. If she don't watch, she'll end up like the old women down Wal Mart, the ones that wear baggy pants and Tea Party t-shirts, can't get round the store without their disabled scooter. Momma was always thin as a minute, reckoned Alice's grandpappy called her Ana cause she was as small as the hummingbird. She blowed up, though, just before the end, on account of the crazy potions and drugs from across the border she took for the cancer cause they didn't have no health insurance. Not by then.

It's not the food that'll make her fat, though; she knows it'll happen, cause she'll just go that way. Aint no reason not to, she reckons. She knows she aint all that happy, aint what they call 'fulfilled', but she don't know nobody who is nowadays. She sees em on reality shows, buncha strangers in a house somewhere, and they all talk about 'finding themselves', but what they mean is finding somebody else, and Alice knows that aint no guarantee of nothing. Hey, she thought she found Charlie. Aint much good come outta that, not since their wedding night when he got drunk and tore her panties off and told her she was gonna do whatever he wanted cause she was his wife, and she was scared but excited at the same time, wanted him so much to do whatever he wanted, and then he passed out.

She woke up next day and it was just the rest of her life.

Roger Hernandez gave her her very first orgasm, though he don't know that. He was working on the ranch, breaking in ponies, and she was watching him from the far gate. The ponies bucked and reared and made such a noise, but Roger Hernandez just held firm, black jeans and shirt and Stetson – colours make em skittish, he told her – and it was like he was the centre of the twisters that whipped by in May, so quiet and still, and she'd felt the safest place in the world must be at the feet of Roger Hernandez. She was sitting astride the gate, the wood hard as iron and bleached in the sun and worn smooth, and without realising it, she'd been working against the hard, hot wood. When she came, it just about knocked her off the fence, like boiling talcum was flowing in her veins, and she wondered if she'd screamed or cried out, but Roger Hernandez just held his pony, calm now, whispering in its ear.

Three months later, Daddy went off to Vegas, lost the ranch in a game of poker and drowned on his own vomit in a cheap motel. He never said a word, just got up early one morning and took the station wagon and that was the last they saw of him. Police came round, asked lots of questions, said they was sorry for their loss, but that didn't stop em causing all sorts of trouble over the body. Died in a whole other state, they said, three state lines to bring him over. Three weeks before they got the body back, in a sealed casket. 'You don't wanna be opening that, ma'm,' said the guy who delivered him back home. 'He'll be mighty ripe.'

Never saw that coming, said Momma, she thought he'd growed outta that, but Alice had seen it sometimes, in the blackness that hung over her Daddy's head when she watched him baling hay in the barn or oiling up his saddle. He'd be quiet and wasn't able to look at her when she called his name; it was like he was collapsing in on himself, like something inside him had died and left an empty space that he was just falling inta, like those black holes in space she'd read about in the *National Geographic* in the library. Then he'd come out of it, but Alice could see, see that some of him had fallen inta that hole and he was never gonna get it back.

She peels and cores the apples. They're a mite old, kinda like rubber balls, only good for pies and the boys won't eat em cause they prefer popsicles and gum even though she keeps telling em it aint good for em. Momma woulda fed em to the ponies, too wrinkled and dry, but prices are getting higher all the time and she can't afford to waste much these days. She likes to do the peeling right, taking the skin off in one long piece, like a ringlet, but the skin's dry and breaks.

The front door opens, bounces back hard on its hinges. Charlie's home. She hears him unpacking himself, the clunk of the CS can, the jingle of his keys, the scrape of the handcuffs, all tossed onto her Momma's butterfly table in the hallway; he'll keep the Glock strapped in its holster awhile, till he gets it in the gun safe. She's asked him a coupla times, be careful with Momma's table, don't scratch it, but he don't seem to pay much mind to her.

By the time he stomps down the hall inta the kitchen, she's buttering up the old pie dish for blind baking, crackle-glazed with bunches of painted cherries. Alice remembers when the men came from the Vegas bank, after Daddy was buried, though she'd never known men who worked for banks who wore bootlace ties, and they said the ranch was theirs, Alice and Momma had to leave. All signed, sealed and delivered said the lawyer, and Momma got just a few sticks of furniture like the butterfly table and her chifferrobe. This pie dish too. Whenever Alice looks at it, she thinks of Buddy Holly.

'Hey hon,' he calls, like he's calling a dog, she thinks. He's all swagger and balls, heads for the refrigerator, wrenches a Bud outta its plastic collar, pops the ringpull, takes a long drink, sighs. Then he looks at her.

'Whatchya doin'?'

'Told the boys I'd make a pie for them coming home from school.'

'Yeah? What kind?'

'Apple.'

'Apple?'

'Yeah.'

'Well, don't be putting too much of that cinnermon in there. I don't like too much of that.'

He leans against the door frame, watching her. He still has it, she reckons, cause for sure the girls still watch him and he watches them watching him and she can tell he likes it, but she can't help thinking he's getting a bit heavy round the middle and his face is puffing up a bit. Cops and donuts, that's what it'll be, cops and donuts.

He loves being a cop. 'Law enforcement officer,' he calls it. Was Charlie who told her about Roger Hernandez. 'Weren't he your daddy's greaser?' he said, and reckoned Roger Hernandez was getting it lucky dying by lethal injection for killing a fellow law enforcement officer. 'Give him to me and the boys at the jailhouse,' he said. 'We'd make him suffer right.'

Charlie shot a Mexican dead once. Traffic bust at three in the morning for breaking a red light. Put two bullets through the guy's head cause when he asked for the licence, the guy went for a gun in the glovebox. Leastways, that's what Charlie and his partner said. Gun in the glovebox was all taped up, no prints, untraceable, just the kinda thing a dealer would have.

Turned out guy was a doctor, though, on his way to the hospital, called in for an emergency. 'Who'da thought it?' said Charlie. 'Shit knows why he went for the gun.' DA didn't press charges, doctor was a loner, no wife nor kids, so it just went away. 'Aint no counting on what greasers'll do,' said Charlie.

That's why she wrote care of the library. Abby don't like Charlie. At their wedding anniversary, last Fall, Alice found em up in the bedroom, she needed ice from the store, wanted to ask Charlie to go geddit, and there was Charlie, his belt unbuckled, and Abby against the far wall, looking scared and angry, and she pushed past Charlie and went back to the party downstairs, if but for a minute before she left. 'Of course you can, honey,' she said, when Alice said how angry Charlie would be.

He leans against the door frame and Alice knows he's got loving on his mind. 'You record the ball game last night?' he says.

'Sure,' she says, 'it's there just waiting for ya.'

'Okay,' he says. 'I'll go watch it.' He stands there, eyeing her.

'Well, go on,' she says.

'Just looking at ma wife,' he says. 'How bout we go upstairs after. Afore the boys get back.'

She sees him, standing there, beer can in one hand, the other hooked in his belt. He has a look like he owns the world, and her in it, all that power in one man. She tries to think what it was she once fell for, but she can't find it, and instead she sees a long, brunette hair caught under his epaulette, curling from his shoulder down around his badge, across his breastbone.

He sees her freeze, follows her eyeline, looks down at the hair. He don't make no move to hide it, though, just looks back up at her until she looks him in the eye, and he just smiles, shrugs like *whatever*.

'So whaddya say?' he says.

She almost jumps out her skin at the sound of his voice. 'What?' she says.

'Keep up, darling. You and me. Upstairs.' He stands offa the door frame, stretches, cricks his neck; she can almost hear his spine crack. 'Have us a little husband and wife time.'

'Okay,' she says, but she sounds like some little mouse down the bottom of a well, and that makes him laugh, short like a bark, and he unbuckles his gunbelt and heads for the TV in the den.

She don't know what she feels, 'cept she feels relieved cause Abby's blonde, so he aint fucking Abby. She'd be disappointed with Abby, she reckons. She always knowed, not for sure, but she knowed, like most women do. Like most women too, she aint ever done nothing bout it. She thinks about her Daddy, so wrapped up in his own troubles he couldn't see the love her momma and her'd had for him, aint no call for killing himself like that, and she thinks bout Roger Hernandez, never put a foot wrong by no woman, and the State of Texas killed him for it.

She'd seen Roger Hernandez around town a lot for a while. Momma and her'd got a little apartment above a convenience store, and Roger Hernandez came by now and again when he'd been fishing or hunting; no, he'd tell Momma, they weren't to think he was giving them charity, no ma'am, he just had too good a day and he couldn't eat all that stuff, and they'd be eating rabbit stew for days, or Momma'd be frying fat carp steaks. Once, he brought some flowers, a big bunch for Momma and a littler bunch for Alice, and she'd changed the water every hour just to keep em alive longer.

Then he got himself hitched, a pretty, smiling Mexican girl, and he held doors open for her and carried their bags everywhere, and Alice hated her till she'd growed up a bit and seen how happy Roger Hernandez was, and they moved to Del Rio and got married. That was the last she'd heard of him until Charlie told her about him killing that trooper.

He was a good man, Roger Hernandez, and Charlie aint, and her Daddy weren't much neither, an she's looking at the pie dish, just about all Daddy left her Momma, and she sends it flying, smashing inta the range and it explodes inta a million pieces. She stands there, looking at what she's done.

Charlie comes barrelling in from the den, face kinda angry and dumb at the same time. 'What's going on, Alice?' he says, real quiet like which is how she always knows he aint for messing with.

'I'm sorry,' she says, 'just clumsy I guess.'

'Clumsy? Looks like you took a hammer to it, woman.'

'Slipped outta my hand,' she says. 'Musta been already cracked to shatter like that.'

'Well, whaddya going to do?'

'Clean it up, I guess. Don't have a pie dish for the apple pie though.'

'Boys'll be disappointed in ya.'

She looks at him, sees the disappointment the boys'll feel already in his face. 'I'd better go get another one. Hardware store by the bus station'll have one. Won't take but twenty minutes.'

He looks up, breathes out like he's trying to keep his patience with her but might not manage it. 'Well, go on then,' he says. 'Hurry up, or we aint gonna get a fuck before they come home.'

He turns away, gets halfway back down the hall before he turns again. 'Alice,' he says.

'Yeah?'

'You be more careful.' He kicks open the door of the den. 'Pie dishes don't grow on trees, ya know.'

She watches the door close behind him. Her purse is hanging on the back door. She feels the air in the house bearing down on her, pressing her chest, so she knows she's better outta it. She goes out the back, round the house; the winda's open on the TV room, she hears the cheering of the crowd, the anchorman going nuts.

The neighbourhood aint what it used to be, even a coupla years ago; the front yards are going to seed, most houses gotta car in the driveway that won't start, aint enough people working to keep them running.

Kids run wild too. Don't come near their place on account of Charlie being a cop, though the Weinbergers from across the street say the boys keep beating up on their kid. She should worry bout the boys, but tell the truth, she reckons she already lost em; she don't see no kindness in em no more.

A cool breeze whips her dress. She looks at the sky, clouds beginning to pile up. A drop of rain splats the ground in front of her like the first frog of a plague dropped from heaven. The hairs on the back of her neck tingle for a second, and she has a recollection of being twelve and sitting astride a gatepost and feeling things her body'd never felt before. She looks up and over the roof of the hardware store, and a jagged fork of lightning cracks down on the TV antenna on the apartment block behind, like the sky's torn open with light from another universe, fizzling the air, and she can almost smell the ozone. Then the thunder rumbles right over her head.

So she's standing outside the hardware store and she's thinking that maybe she won't go in cause the bus station's right next door, and those songs of other places keep running through her head.

And, hey, those pie dishes? Well, they don't grow on trees.

Em Strang

COMING OF AGE
For F

When the light finally comes,
a single ray at the curtain's edge,

the girl moves over
and takes it in her hand.

She listens to it crackle, the soft split
of the sun-pulse, the open ache.

She wraps the light carefully
in the deep folds of her bed,

climbs in after it,
glows.

Laura Tansley

IN SOME PLACES, AT THIRTEEN, YOU CAN OWN A GUN

The rap on the door made Nora tense up, interrupting the stream of her pee.

'Is there someone there?'

Nora wasn't sure if she should answer, not sure from which direction the voice had come.

'There's no loo roll in here, could you pass some under?'

Four fingers slid under the gap on the right-hand side of her cubicle; long, strong-sounding nails tapped the plastic-coated wood waiting for an answer. Nora took one, two, three sheets, then thought to take four, five, six from the dispenser. She didn't say anything, but reached down and let the searching hand take the paper.

'Lovely, thank you.'

She waited for the noise from the flush of the neighbouring toilet before unclenching, then took her time pulling up her tights and straightening her skirt.

When she left the cubicle the woman was drying her hands. The mulchy smell of discarded wet paper towels made the bathroom a cold, damp mess.

'Hello Nora, I didn't realise it was you.'

It was Aunty Cath. Nora hadn't noticed her either, but she thought it would be smarter not to admit this.

'Hello Aunty Cath.'

'How are you?' Cath asked, 'How are you finding all this today?'

'It's okay.'

'Mmm, a bit boring for you, I bet. You look very nice though.'

Nora's mum had helped her pick out the outfit: a white skirt with big purple flowers, her patent school shoes, and a cardigan that was made of something very soft that got darker when you stroked it one way, lighter in the other.

'Do you like my hair?' Cath asked, 'I've just had it cut.'

'It looks nice.'

'I thought I'd go a bit shorter this time.'

Aunty Cath's hair was light brown and frizzy from too much dye and too many perms. It looked brittle like Easter birdnest treats. She'd had a fringe cut since the last time Nora had seen her, swooping stylishly to the side, but she wore the same oversized plastic glasses that she'd had forever, resting on her tiny, upturned nose and covering most of her face.

Aunty Cath was one of those aunties who may or may not have been related to her. A second or third cousin of her mother's, it was possible she was so distant that it didn't matter. Cath had lived with Uncle Tony on Beauchamp Avenue, the road directly behind theirs, since before Nora could remember. Uncle Tony was a sheep-farmer. He owned a small flock in a field out past the railway lines and he used to let Nora run around there, herd the sheep and climb on the hay bales even though her mum had told her she could slip between two stacks and suffocate. They'd split up suddenly, him and Cath; one day they were together, the next Uncle Tony's car was gone and Nora had never seen him again. Uncle Tony took the pets (a cat, a dog and the carp from the pond) and Cath kept the house, for a while. She'd called one evening soon after they'd split to ask Nora's dad to come round and get the shotgun Tony kept in the attic. She didn't want it in the house, and didn't want him coming back to get it. She said at the time that she didn't think he'd use it, but break-ups did funny things to people, she'd seen it happen before. Nora remembered Cath's face that day: pink with thrill, twitching. She was like an animal that had learned to limp. Aunty Cath lived somewhere else now, sometimes with, sometimes without a boyfriend. Uncle Tony became Tony, someone they all used to know and pray they'd never run in to.

Cath opened her mouth to say something but the hand-dryer chose that moment to sense something and switch on and anything she said was lost under the sound of the warm air that Nora let blast 'til her hands were red. The water from the taps had been icy; the frosted pipes and the single-glazing chilling the contents of the bathroom, crisping the flowers on the ledge and turning her fingers white. But the dryer stopped again suddenly and no amount of waving seemed to be able to turn it back on.

Cath was rummaging through the contents of her purse by the mirrors. The clatter of dainty plastic cases of makeup, mirrors, keys and jewellery gently jostling each other sounded soothing and sophisticated. Cath found her lipstick and drew colour in a circle from her bottom lip and around, then dabbed at the place between her eyebrows with a triangular sponge that was white on one side, orange-beige on the other.

She must have noticed Nora staring because she asked, 'do you want to borrow some?'

Nora moved forward.

'Shall I?' Cath offered, and picked up the little cases before Nora had got near enough to touch them.

With one hand holding her chin, tilting her face up towards the bare striplights that shone blue in their centres, Cath dabbed at Nora's bottom lip with the stick, soft and creamy like a crayon.

'Take this,' Cath passed a tissue to Nora, soft and fluffy from age, and she put it between her lips leaving her own smaller kiss on one of its edges, the lines of her lip-creases like the veins of a leaf.

Next Cath took the compact and pressed a catch revealing a compartment and three colours: pink, brown and gold. There was a brush lying flat and perpendicular to the powders whose edges splayed out, stiff from overuse. Cath ran the brush vigorously over all three colours then swept Nora's cheeks back towards her ears twice on each side. Cath's hands smelt of too many things: talcum powder, tangerines and a pop-star fragrance.

'There, what do you think?'

Nora saw the bright colour through the water-spots on the mirrors and thought it made her look fake somehow, like a moustache drawn on the face of a statue.

'It really suits you,' Cath said.

Nora wasn't sure if it did or didn't, but she liked it.

'How old are you now?' Cath asked.

'Thirteen,' Nora said. She regarded the transition to teen like a trophy. There was a clear difference between her and the new First Years at school now. They looked tiny on their first day and she had laughed at the clueless girls that wore white ankle socks and school-approved skirts down to their knees. They didn't know, didn't realise, and it only took a few days before they were wearing tights and rolling their skirts up at the waist but it was too late. They'd been marked out.

'Mmm,' Cath said putting the lid back on the lipstick with a firm click, 'I'm sure you'd rather be in town on a Saturday, chasing boys and shopping, eh? Do you have a boyfriend?'

'No-no-no,' Nora went red despite the fact she had nothing to hide.

'Oh I see. Anyone you like though?'

She wasn't sure. Maybe.

'I remember what it was like, all very exciting. Meeting boys and going out on dates. I bet most of your friends are having sex aren't they.'

'No,' she shook her head quickly.

'Well maybe they are and they're just not telling you.'

There were rumours, of other older, different girls in her year. On the common with someone's brother, in a tent over in the fields by Cowleigh Park, with someone from a different school. But no one she knew had ever even been alone with a boy at night.

'They aren't,' she said again, hitting the 't' hard so Cath would know who was right and who was wrong.

Cath smiled and folded her arms across her chest pulling down the olive-green sweater she was wearing 'til Nora could see the scalloped lace at the top of her white bra and wrinkled lines of skin reaching down the line of her cleavage.

'Well make sure everyone plays safe won't you, don't want anyone getting in trouble. Not like your old Aunty Cath. Are you and your friends being safe?'

'We don't, I'm not …'

'Let me give you something,' Cath grabbed her purse and stuck her nose deep in to it as if she was foraging for food.

'I don't need—'

'Nonsense, here take them,' and she offered two foil-silver squares that were attached along one side with a perforated seam.

'It's okay, I'm fine,' Nora held up a hand to stop her from coming closer.

Cath was poised on her toes like she might make a grab for Nora's purse.

Instead she grabbed Nora's wrist, 'Here,' and put the little packets in her palm, forcing her fingers closed around them.

Nora opened the clasp of her bag and shoved them in without looking at them. They'd felt cold and slick and the sharp foil scratched the lining of her empty bag, a noise her dad was sure to hear from wherever. She'd hide them somewhere, maybe at Rachel's house. She had a bigger bedroom with more dookits and drawers. She'd slept there all of last weekend. They'd bought a book of spells from the New Age place in town and had sat at two a.m. watching films with fingers touching the edge of a dinner plate filled with tea lights chanting the names of boys they liked, boys they hated. She wondered now what Rachel could have hid in the shadows.

'You don't want to catch anything do you, all sorts of nasty stuff out there. Warts and sores and what not. And you don't want any unexpected arrivals either.'

Nora hadn't even got her period. Rachel had got hers in the summer. And she'd spoken once, the first time it happened, about the tenderness in her back and boobs, ripples of aches across her stomach, its sludgy starts to the rouge-slick shock of it in full flow. But she didn't bring it up any more.

'I was pregnant once. A complete mistake. Thank goodness I lost it,' Cath was fussing with her hair, prodding her fringe, mussing her scalp and creating static from its dryness that made her split-ends fizzle, 'I never found the right time for kids, never found that I ever wanted them more than I didn't want them. One list was always longer than the other. Would you like kids?'

'I don't know.'

'Well you've got to decide now really, because it changes everything. You have to lose things. Most things that you want will have to go, out of your plans.'

'Mum got things she wanted.'

'Mmm,' she murmured flatly.

She looked at Nora in the mirror for a second, then quickly walked the length of the bathroom pushing the door of each stall open, to check the gaps for two eyes looking back, for feet planted flat or fingers folded in a lap.

Turning back to Nora, breathing in all the air around her, she said, 'Maybe your mum didn't get the things she wanted. Maybe your mum wanted a whole mess of things but she had you kids to look after and that meant she had to give things up, put things away. I knew her before you came along, remember.'

'Like what? Like what did she want?'

'I don't know, anything. Everything, maybe. But it had to be that way, couldn't be any other, and that's that.' She looked at Nora, trying to impress the point, 'Matthew and I, you know, my boyfriend, we spoke about it, just yesterday in fact, but we knew the answers already. He's lovely actually, did I tell you? He's very young. Much too young for me. Strawberry-blonde like rhubarb and custard. I could ask if he knows anyone for you if you like. Or you could have him after me,' she laughed a little, but her heavy eyelids stayed low and testing.

Nora stared passed Cath to the *faux*-marble counter and let her eyes relax. The white-grey flecks of the imitation surface, the dark reds and sun-bleached browns of the dried-out flowers clenching at the cold seeping in through the windows whose frames were warped and chipped and a colour that used to be yellow; the barely there colours faded into something even duller.

'I've got some wrinkle cream here if you'd like some,' she waved a small, blue tube by its end, 'got it free with a makeup bag. Never too young to start, you know.'

She dropped the tube next to the sink, pushed the pink toilet door and walked out letting it swing back and forth. Noise from the hall was fanned in 'til it came to rest: the chilly echoes of conversations, cold cuts and lukewarm coffee unhindered by thin walls and worn carpets. Nora knew there was a space heater next to the kitchen where the sandwiches were getting their crusts cut and turned into triangles. She could stand next to it and let the orange bars warm her legs 'til the hairs there started to prickle, pretending to have a job that required her to be near the door, away from the buffet tables where people lingered. But that cranky old heater spewed out angry heat unimpeded by a guard. She knew it from other funerals, other birthdays of other people she didn't really know and who were too old to really know her. It might melt her plastic purse, heating the foil of Aunty Cath's cast-offs 'til they crackled and burnt like fire-pit jacket potatoes. She'd ignite and they'd have to put her out with the ratty red fire blankets the community hall had kept for emergencies since the blitz. And while they were rolling her around, patting her down, they'd see the melted makeup on her face, see what was in her bag and they'd glare at her, then they'd try to have a serious talk with her. Another serious talk. She got angry again and found her voice.

'She's talking shit.'

The word sounded awkward as she said it, coming out more like 'shirt' because of how she'd pushed the consonants out, unused to their shapes. It didn't suit her, and the cold, wet bathroom tiles bounced the word back like the slapping sound of a soggy-charlie thrown against a wall, or palms hitting the ground to break a fall.

Sheila Templeton

DUMFOONERT

Ye huv tae ken – I wis eleeven year auld
– hine awa fae onything resemblin
wummanhood. It wis the smells –
the burnt spun-sugar, iley flattened girse
the reek-boak fae their caravans;
canvas creakin as the nicht daurkened
an the bricht lichts o the hale carnival
birled aboon ma heid, lik jewels.
I hudnae a thocht o findin a jo
nor a jo o findin me. So faan the mannie
offered free tickets tae the early show –
there wis me an Davie, Ally an Sandy,
my compadres o the summer
my burn guddlin, bosky-wood explorin
best freens – we thankit him an slippit in
richt doon at the front, swellin the numbers
as nae doot wis the intention – tae find –
Estelle the Tassel Swinger.
Left rotation, right rotation
then baith at eence, the glint o gold
swingin, skiry, dazzlin.
Nae a fustle, nae a wheeber
escaped oor lips as we watched,
dumfoonert, thirlt tae the spectacle;
nae a single carnal thocht
in ony heid. Jist gaap-mou admiration.
Fit wye is she able tae dee that?
Even the big loons at the back kept their gabs shut
in the face o sic saik-less wunner.

GLESGA FAIR

She's goat her legs oot –
her foldin plastic chair
oan the gress at Glesga Green –
an her airms an enough
creamy dimpled bosom
tae please Renoir;
bra straps oan show,
frock lirkit richt up
ower her knees
sittin lik a mannie
legs weel splayed as if
tae accommodate
magnificent baws –
but it's no that.
It's tae mak room
mak a space
for her belly,
lovely big roon
wumman's belly
growthie in the sun.

Alan Trotter

THE ASTONISHING HOLCOMB
(An extract from the novel Muscle*)*

The poker games began to happen weekly, sometimes twice a week. Normally just with _____, the apartment manager and Lydia. They'd play and when the apartment manager or Lydia took a break I'd sit in for them, or else Lydia would show me her hands, or else I'd just sleep and never mind the game in the other room. One night a scrawny kid joined them – a writer for the pulps, Holcomb, who the apartment manager knew from the track.

The kid was of the sort that he'd hold his cigarettes only in ways that didn't quite make sense, like he'd over-thought the whole exercise and grown worried it wouldn't be impressive enough just to hold it like a damn cigarette.

To begin with he talked plenty. It was a friendly game and the chips were pretty sociable, passing the time with everybody in turn. But the kid, holding his cigarette at a complicated angle and talking a lot without saying much, when he'd win a stack, his face would color with pride and his back would straighten out – his dignity standing to attention. It was like seeing a corpse jump to its feet and give itself a round of applause.

When this would happen Lydia would tell a joke, distracting from the display, because she's a good one and it was embarrassing watching the kid win.

Then the kid started getting bad hands and kept playing them. It was clear they were bad because he gummed up. He was still okay in chips but he wasn't talking. He wasn't even laughing at Lydia's jokes and she tells a dirty joke as well as anyone you ever knew. But he would raise and lose and get dealt more bad cards and his back would crimp, the sad reverse of the military posture he'd get when he was winning.

You could have beaten him at cards if you were dead drunk in a dark room as long as you had a protractor to take the angle of his spine.

The kid, the Astonishing Holcomb, became a regular. He played cards and he drank and he never seemed to get better at either. And he talked, which he could do.

There was one hand late in an evening where Holcomb was almost out of his chair with excitement right from the deal, but the apartment manager was too drunk to notice. Lydia had one arm across her belly, the other pressing a black cigarette to her lips, the lips much more red than normal. She was in kind of a mean mood, where sometimes the day after a mood like this and with her husband on a drunk, you'd see him wondering what he'd done to get almost markless but professionally painful wounds on his arms, and on one occasion a cigarette burn in the center of his back, up between his shoulder blades, right where he couldn't reach it or quite see it properly so it had him running out his door whenever he heard feet on the steps to get someone else to take a look and give him word on what exactly was back there.

So Lydia began laughing at the apartment manager as he kept raising, laughing that he couldn't see the kid Holcomb's excitement. Holcomb is helium at this point, his bright eyes all the way up by the ceiling. He was too flush with excitement to care about Lydia laughing, and the apartment manager was too far gone to pay any attention to her anyway.

And of course it ended as a big win for Holcomb. Though it's less a win for the player than it is for the cards, in this instance.

He raked the chips to himself and then lighted a new cigarette, and as the next hand was being dealt he gave a wave over his part of the table like a magician over a coin trick that meant he wanted dealt out.

And while the other three played the hand, he started to talk about the story of Red Riding Hood, which I'd heard, and the Grimm brothers, who he seemed to think were quite the deal but were news to the rest of the table. He said that in the story of Red Riding Hood a little girl has been sent through the woods to visit her sick grandmother. And a bad wolf knows this, because he speaks to Little Red Riding Hood, and for some reason she gives him the straight tip on it. And the wolf goes ahead to grandma's house and eats the old lady and dresses in her old lady night-clothes and climbs into her bed and waits for Red Riding Hood.

Lydia showed me the low pair in her hand and then folded it to a modest raise from _____. She picked up her cigarette and said that she didn't know about the rest of the table but she'd had a childhood and parents and – (she drew a circle with the smoke to say, and so on). She seems older when she's in a mean mood. She tells fewer jokes, though they're just as funny. I was thinking I might take a glass of milk and go get some sleep.

Holcomb took a draw on his pill and piped the smoke thinly from the corner of his mouth, taking his time.

And according to the Grimm brothers, Red Riding Hood arrives and admires the wolf's eyes and ears and teeth, and the wolf eats her up, and then a hunter comes by. And the hunter cuts open the wolf with a scissors and gets little Red Riding Hood and the grandma out, and piles rocks into the wolf in their place, and then sews the wolf up again. And it's having a belly full of rocks that does for the wolf in The End.

Lydia pushed her chips into the apartment manager's pile, and sat back to smoke her cigarette and watch _____ and the apartment manager play. They came to an agreement over how quickly the blinds would go up.

But, Holcomb says, the wolf's still lucky. Even the wolf in the next story, that no one remembers, the wolf that ends drowned in grandma's gutter chasing the sausage smell of cooking water is lucky. Because a twist like Red Riding Hood is always going to find a story to be a part of – some characters just have adventures thrown at them – but what's so special about a big, dumb animal, with big teeth and big claws and no sense? And the grandma – if she didn't have little Red Riding Hood as an affectionate, selfless granddaughter, what are the chances she'd get to be in any stories? She'd just be an old woman, sick and bed-bound, alone in the woods.

The poker game was settling into a steady rhythm, the apartment manager and _____ passing the cards and their blinds back and forth – shuffle, deal, fold, shuffle, deal, like they were doing it in their sleep, or like they were doing it in mine. No one spoke apart from Holcomb – no one else had any room to speak or think the way Holcomb was speaking.

So, another version of the story, Holcomb says: Red Riding Hood's on her way to grandma's, and the wolf talks to her and then goes on ahead and devours grandma, but Red Riding Hood is distracted by another adventure, another story going on in the other direction through the woods, with a witch, or brothers turned into swans, or some bears instead of a big cruel wolf. So the wolf waits in bed, in grandma's night-clothes, with the grandma's sheets pulled up to its neck, but Red Riding Hood doesn't come.

'And after waiting for so long in the too-small bed,' he goes on, 'the wolf's back begins to hurt, so, as he scours the shelves of the house for something to eat, he finds that he's begun to walk with a stoop. And as winter draws in, his feet are always sore, and he has to rub them before trying to stand. And the wolf's big eyes are no longer as good for seeing anything with, and the wolf's ears can barely hear the wind whipping at the walls of the cottage, and the wolf's teeth hurt whenever he bites anything until he's glad when one would fall out. And soon the wolf has no appetite at all and the grandma-nightclothes that used to bind his legs they were so tight, they hang loosely on him. And the wolf comes to think of himself as living in another wood, a wood within the cottage within the wood, an interior wood where each tree is another ache somewhere in his old body, and all the trees grow unnoticeably bigger day by day by day. Still his granddaughter hasn't come to bring him some cake or a bottle of wine. His hair is matted and thinned, and sometimes in the morning he finds clumps of it in his bed, which he tidies, because it's important to keep the place nice, even if no one is coming.

'Still the forest of aches in the wolf grows bigger and its branches entwine, and he forgets ever living anywhere but in its dull pains and occasional sharp agonies in his small cottage, as his memory fades and dims.'

*

One night there was another card game, larger than usual, with seven players. _____, Lydia, a Greek barber who lived in the building, an ex-buzzer called Palmer, a few others. The writer was there, Holcomb.

He made it clear that he'd just been paid, talking about it and then, when that didn't get the acclaim he wanted, taking the money from his pocket and fanning it for us all to admire.

But now he had some money, for the first time he didn't seem to have any interest in losing it. He made himself comfortable in his chair, sitting out as many hands as he played.

In one hand he folded his cards before the flop, then pulled from beneath the table a small calfskin case that looked new and opened with a snap. From the case he took some wine glasses, enough for everyone at the table. A red scale curved inside each base, a wine stain. He took a bottle from the case and half-filled the glasses with whisky, good stuff.

Then he sat back and swirled his glass lazily and started talking. His subject was how much he liked getting paid, and particularly how much he liked getting paid by the word.

He talked about it for a long time. If he meant it to sound like he was someone who made a lot of money, he didn't. It went the other way. If he was a musician he'd have been on knee sweetly serenading a half-dollar up in her bed chamber. But he was a talker.

After he'd spoken for a long time about the various feelings having some money in his pocket gave him, he went quiet for a while, sipping his whisky. The whole table was in the kind of silence that comes when nobody's getting the cards they feel they deserve.

Holcomb had reached the point in the bottle and the evening where his glass butted against his mouth when he lifted it and drops of liquor slid down his chin, and when he set it on the table more slopped over the side. He said,

'The beautiful thing about being paid by the word is that it supplies us with an exchange rate between reality and language. Wait, no, that's getting ahead of myself, that is abrupt and ugly, a dull edge. We shouldn't allow dull and brutal things when we speak any more than we would when we write,' he said looking at me – I guess because I was the only person still giving him the attention he wanted. I'd been coming and going from the table so I hadn't been as subject to it as everyone else. Now I was sitting in for Lydia, about to fold low suited connectors. I'd left for her the glass of whisky he'd pushed at me.

Lydia was smoking a black cigarette by the open window, looking out at the street. The apartment manager was out and she didn't know where. If anyone at the table knew they were too kind to tell her.

'The beautiful thing about being paid by the word,' said Holcomb, 'is – well, let's say all my money comes from my writing and all the writing I do is paid by the word. I write for the love pulps mainly. Terrible things, too coy even to have the dignity of the earnestly seedy. Some science fiction too.

'Now obviously you could go through my apartment, and for each of my belongings you could attach a label with the dollar value of that item. I paid this much for the typewriter, this much for the desk, this much for the brandy. Now each word I write I get paid two cents. Sometimes it's less than that, sometimes it's even a bit more. But let's say two cents. If you know how many cents I paid for something you could figure out a word that I've sold the necessary number of times to pay for that thing.

'Now we've got a new set of labels for my belongings. It's not a number and a dollar sign. The scotch is labelled 'suddenly'. The typewriter's got the label 'lusting'. There's plenty of lusting in love pulps. But the desk's even more expensive, so it's labelled with a pronoun maybe, or a conjunction. Perhaps 'because' is enough to buy the desk. I see your 'rugged' and raise you 'wistful'!' he said and threw a couple of chips into the pot, though he'd folded the hand without even looking at his cards. _____ gave him a look and the kid pulled them back, being careful not to disturb the pile. Only two players – _____ and Palmer – were still in the pot. Palmer had got early retirement from the force when he was photographed selling guns out the back of his prowl car. We'd met him when _____ and I had to break his hand over a small debt. They carried on playing. _____ called a raise and dealt another card. Holcomb drew on his cigarette with a look of great concentration.

_____ took the pot. He passed the deck to the man to his left to deal the next hand.

'What's beautiful about being paid by the word,' said Holcomb, 'is that we know exactly what everyone in this room is worth.' He crossed his arms and took another drag on his smoke. 'Assuming that they're worth anything,' he said. He was offered a card and rejected it, and the game carried on without him. I got another bum hand and folded to a low raise.

From the window, Lydia said, 'What's horrible about low-rent writers being paid by the word, is that they feel the need to keep going on even when they've run out of things to say.'

'Think about how many words anyone's going to spend describing you,' Holcomb carried on, looking at her. 'Maybe your beau's right now composing sonnets instead of at a leg show or haggling prices for a lay. Could be. And maybe Mrs Palmer's at home filling notebooks with beautiful similes, pages and pages of heartfelt whimsy.'

'There ain't no Mrs Palmer,' said Palmer, though I don't think Holcomb heard him. 'Not presently, leastways.' Lydia smoked her black cigarette and looked out at the empty street however people look at things that don't mean anything.

I nearly said something to all this, but I couldn't find the words or the energy. If Lydia had been the kind to take offence I might have worked harder at it.

'Let's suppose they are! Right this moment – they're hard at work behind a pile of hitherto unexpressed affection and rhyming dictionaries. Unimportant – it doesn't matter. What I mean is, how many words would it take to plumb the depths? How many cents before they, or anyone else who might turn their pen to the task, have scraped bare the walls of the soul they've set out to describe?'

To the right of Palmer sat a dog handler. He was by nature a bit less animated than an old Irish Basset who didn't get excited for much of anything since its owners had it put down. All night he'd kept his hat on, the smoke from a stub of a cigar catching and then deflecting on the brim, so it tumbled up like a waterfall upended. The cigar rolled around one side of his mouth and he pushed in half his chips.

The only others left in were me and _____. I called, _____ folded. Palmer laid another card on the table. The old dog handler didn't raise his old runny eyes, just pushed in the rest of his chips, worked his cigar with his big jaw. I called, and looked round to find Lydia had turned from the window and moved towards the game, watching as I doubled her chips, which felt good. When I'd turned my cards to show to the droopy hound, I looked to her and she smiled at me, a small smile like it was something she'd whispered, so just I'd catch it. The dog handler took his jacket from the back of his chair, straightened his hat on his head, nodded to the room and left.

Holcomb watched the door close behind the dog handler. 'A paragraph and a half? Maybe two? What's that, Two hundred words? Two cents a word gives us two dollars for a hundred words. So four bucks,' he said and turned around to look at Palmer, then Lydia, then at the Greek barber. 'How much for this whole room? How much for you, loogan?' he said to me, a loogan being a guy who carries a gun. I stood up and he drew back as if I'd pulled one on him, and Lydia took her seat at the table. Holcomb lighted a cigarette, trying to look casual. 'How many words for you, Box?' he said again. I filled my glass at the tap and sat and watched the game for a while longer. I didn't even own a rod. Neither did _____.

After he'd quit talking, Holcomb found himself in a room where all there was for him to do was lose money, but still not in a mood to do it. Losing he could do when it made him feel a victim, but the bills in his wallet were too big a cushion for him to be anything but comfortable, at least in a small stakes game like this. And he was all but incapable of winning.

If only he hadn't been so lousy at cards. It must have been bittersweet for him – a writer that easy to read.

I didn't think of that line, that's something someone else used on him once at the table. A good one.

Hamish Whyte

LION

Walking up from the river
the flood defence man
in his orange helmet
    and yellow high-vis jacket
whistles back to the blackbird
singing out from the cherry blossom.
A cat pads past and the trill
turns to warning.
'That cat,' the man says to his mate,
'is a lion.'
There's a breeze
and petals drift down
    like flakes of snow.

BIOGRAPHIES

Gregor Addison lives in Glasgow and has published in *New Writing Scotland, Chapman, Causeway/Cabhsair,* the *Edinburgh Review, Gairm, Gath,* and the *Scotsman*. His poems were included in the Carcanet *Oxford Poet's Anthology 2013* and he is currently putting the finishing touches to his first collection of poetry.

Claire Askew's poetry has appeared in various publications including the *Guardian, Poetry Scotland,* the *Edinburgh Review, The Feminist Wire, PANK* and *Popshot*. Her work has also won numerous accolades including the inaugural International Salt Prize for Poetry (2013), the Virginia Warbey Poetry Prize (2010) and a Scottish Book Trust New Writers Award (2012). Claire holds a PhD in Creative Writing and Contemporary Women's Poetry from the University of Edinburgh, and blogs at **onenightstanzas.com**

Paul Brownsey has been a newspaper reporter and a lecturer in philosophy at Glasgow University. His stories have appeared in most of the literary magazines of Scotland and also in England, Ireland and North America – most recently in the 2014 edition of the long-running American series *Best Gay Romance*.

Ron Butlin is a former Edinburgh Makar. *The Sound of My Voice* has won several international prizes and was included in the Guardian's 1000 Books You Have To Read. His latest novel, *Ghost Moon*, was published this spring. Ron lives in Edinburgh with his wife, the writer Regi Claire. **www.ronbutlin.co.uk**

Martin Connor lives and works in the northwest of Glasgow and was a co-founder of the Edwin Morgan International Poetry Competition. He enjoys finishing poems.

George Craig's stories have been published in *From Glasgow to Saturn* and *Tip Tap Flat*, placed runner-up in the *Guardian* Short Story Competition and shortlisted for the Bridport Prize. He holds law degrees from Glasgow and NYU, completed Faber Academy's novel writing course and graduated with distinction from Glasgow University's MLitt. He has recently finished his first novel.

Seth Crook taught philosophy at various universities before deciding to move to the Hebrides. He does not like cod philosophy in poetry, but likes cod, philosophy and poetry. His poems have recently appeared in a number of fine online poetry magazines and in print in *Gutter, Magma, The Rialto, Orbis, Envoi, Interpreter's House, Other Poetry, The SHOp, Northwords Now, The Journal, Southlight.*

Anna Crowe is a poet, creative-writing tutor, and translator of Catalan and Mexican poetry. She is co-founder and former Artistic Director of StAnza, Scotland's International Poetry Festival. A Callum Macdonald Memorial Award-winner, her poetry and translations have been Poetry Book Society Choices, and in 2005 she received a Travelling Scholarship from the Society of Authors.

Ever Dundas is a writer and artist specialising in the weird and macabre. She graduated from Edinburgh Napier University with a Masters in Creative Writing with Distinction, and her interests include Queer Theory and the relationship between humans and animals. You can delve into her strange world here: **bloodonforgottenwalls.wordpress.com**

David Eyre is a writer and journalist. He was born in Coatbridge in 1972, spent his high school years in Glasgow, studied Scottish literature and Gaelic at Edinburgh University, and now lives in Dunbar. His poems have been published in *Poetry Scotland, Irish pages, Northwords Now, An Guth* and *Gutter.*

Olivia Ferguson was born in Lanark. She has spent the last several years in Canada, living in Vancouver, Montréal, Victoria, and Calgary. She is about to begin a PhD in English Literature at the University of Edinburgh, and continues working on her novel, *The Swim.*

Originally from Edinburgh, **Alison Flett** moved to Adelaide, South Australia in 2010. Her poetry collection *Whit Lassyz Ur Inty* (Thirsty Books, 2004) was shortlisted for the Saltire Book of the Year Award. Last year she won the South Australian Satura Prize for poetry and came second in the West Australian Glen Phillips Poetry Prize.

Graham Fulton was born in 1959 and lives in Paisley. His five full-length poetry collections have been published by Polygon, Smokestack Books,

Red Squirrel Press and The Grimsay Press. A new collection, *One Day in the Life of Jimmy Denisovich*, is to be published by Smokestack in 2014.

Charlie Gracie is from Baillieston, Glasgow and now lives near Stirling. His work, featured in many Scottish publications, is about dark places and the glimmer that lives there and about green places and what lies beyond the surface. He often collaborates with other visual, sound and creative artists.

George Gunn is from Thurso in Caithness, where he lives. In 2013 he published his eighth book of poems, *A Northerly Land*. He has had over fifty plays produced for stage and radio since 1984. He writes the 'From the Province of the Cat' column for the magazine *Bella Caledonia*.

Mark Harding recently competed an MA in Creative Writing at Edinburgh Napier University. He lives in Edinburgh and is a member of the spoken word collective Writers' Bloc. Mark is working on a collection of stories about the impact of IT on our lives.

Gail Honeyman lives and works in Glasgow, and writes drama and fiction.

Alison Irvine's novel, *This Road is Red* (Luath Press), was shortlisted for the 2011 Saltire First Book of the Year award. She is currently working on a Glasgow Life Commonwealth Games commission, *The Winning City*, collaborating with film-maker Chris Leslie and illustrator Mitch Miller. **www.thewinningcity.co.uk**

Brian Johnstone's work has appeared throughout Scotland, in the UK, north America and Europe. He has published six collections, his latest being *Dry Stone Work* (Arc, 2014). Later in 2014 his work will be appearing on The Poetry Archive website. He has appeared at various international poetry festivals from Macedonia to Nicaragua, and at venues across the UK. **brianjohnstonepoet.co.uk**

David Kinloch hails from Glasgow. He is the author of five books of poetry, most recently *Finger of a Frenchman* (Carcanet, 2011). He currently teaches poetry and creative writing at the University of Strathclyde.

Helen Lamb has published a collection of poetry, *Strange Fish* (Duende), and a short story collection, *Superior Bedsits* (Polygon). She is a Royal

Literary Fund advisory fellow and also teaches creative writing at the University of Edinburgh's Office of Lifelong Learning. She lives in Dunblane.

Marcas Mac an Tuairneir was born in York and studied Gaelic at the University of Aberdeen. His début collection of poetry – *Deò* – was published in 2013. He lives in Inverness where he is a member of Inverness Gaelic Choir and is Internet and Informations Officer at Bòrd na Gàidhlig.

Richie McCaffery lives in Stirling and teaches and studies at the University of Glasgow where he is a PhD student in Scottish Literature. His pamphlet collections are *Spinning Plates* (HappenStance Press, 2012) and *Ballast Flint* (Cromarty Arts Trust, 2013). His first book-length collection is forthcoming from Nine Arches Press in June 2014.

James McGonigal is a poet, editor and translator, formerly a school teacher and educationalist. He is currently editing *The Midnight Letterbox: Selected Correspondence of Edwin Morgan 1950–2010*, to be published by Carcanet Press in 2015. His last collection, *Cloud Pibroch* (Mariscat Press, 2010), won the UK Michael Marks Poetry Pamphlet Award.

Crìsdean MacIlleBhàin / Christopher Whyte's fifth collection, *An Daolag Shìonach*, with new poems from 2004 to 2007 and uncollected poems from 1987 to 1999, was published by Glasgow University Celtic Department in October 2013. His translations of Marina Tsvetaeva's lyrical poems from 1918 to 1920 will appear in New York next August as *Moscow in the Plague Year*. He is a full-time writer, living between Venice and Budapest.

Martin MacInnes has published fiction and reportage in several magazines including *Edinburgh Review 134* and *138*. He read at the Edinburgh International Book Festival in 2013, and won a New Writers Award from the Scottish Book Trust in 2014. His long project is about natural history and identity.

Mary McIntosh, retired teacher, lives in Kirriemuir. Writes mainly in Scots. Published in *New Writing Scotland*, *Lallans*, and *Riverrun*, also various anthologies including *A Tongue in Yer Heid*. Ketillonia has published *The Gless Hoose* , a pamphlet of her short stories. Now writes short plays for a local street theatre group.

Hugh McMillan is an award-winning poet from Penpont in Dumfries and Galloway in Scotland who has been published and anthologised widely. He is currently working on a book commissioned by the Wigtown Book Festival, a sequel to *MacTaggarts Gallovidian Encyclopaedia* of 1824.

Kevin MacNeil is an award-winning writer from Stornoway, now living in London. Books include *Love and Zen in the Outer Hebrides* (Canongate), *The Stornoway Way* (Penguin) and *A Method Actor's Guide to Jekyll and Hyde* (Polygon). He has lectured in creative writing at the universities of Uppsala, Edinburgh and Kingston. Practising Buddhist. Dedicated cyclist, avid reader, but never at the same time. **www.kevinmacneil.com**

Robin Fulton Macpherson's translations of Tomas Tranströmer and Harry Martinson have been published by Bloodaxe Books (the Martinson volume winning the Bernard Shaw Prize for Translation from Swedish for 2012), and of Kjell Espmark by Marick Press (Michigan). Marick Press has recently brought out his own *A Northern Habitat: Collected Poems 1960–2010*.

Gillian Mayes is an academic gone over to the other side, having recently graduated with an M.Litt. in Creative Writing (Glasgow University). She has written a great deal, starting at aged eleven with diaries which had to be abandoned when her children learned to read.

Philip Murnin is from Pollokshields in the south side of Glasgow. He works for Citizens Advice and in his spare time, he writes. This year, he's a recipient of a New Writers Award and will soon finish his first novel, *Phoenixland*. He's a member of G2 Writers who run a Wednesday writers' workshop at the Art Club.

Niall O'Gallagher's first book of poems, *Beatha Ùr*, was published by Clàr in 2013. He lives in Glasgow.

A selection of **Chris Powici**'s poems, *Somehow This Earth*, was published by Diehard in 2009. He edits *Northwords Now* magazine, teaches creative writing for the University of Stirling and the Open University and enjoys a happy addiction to cycling.

Maggie Rabatski is a Harriswoman who lives in Glasgow. She has published two poetry pamphlet collections, *Down From The Dance/An Dèidh An*

Dannsa and *Holding*, both with New Voices Press. She is a previous mentee of the Clydebuilt poetry mentoring scheme and writes in both Gaelic and English.

Cynthia Rogerson has written four novels and collection of short stories. Her work has been shortlisted for prizes, translated into seven languages and broadcast on BBC radio. She won the VS Pritchett Prize in 2007.

Andrew Sclater is a poet, actor and drystane dyker from Edinburgh. He has previously edited Darwin's letters, restored historic gardens, and grown flowers for the queen. His poetry has won new writers' awards from the Scottish Book Trust, and New Writing North. Andrew was shortlisted for the Picador Poetry Prize.

Helen Sedgwick won a Scottish Book Trust New Writers Award in 2012, and her writing has been published internationally and broadcast on BBC Radio 4. She works as Managing Director of Cargo Publishing and Managing Editor of Gutter. Say hello at **helensedgwick.com**

Emma Sedlak is a Scottish–American poet whose work has previously appeared in literary journals such as *Crannog, Quiddity*, and *The South Carolina Review*. She is currently completing her PhD in Creative Writing at the University of Edinburgh, and has been a finalist in the Dorothy Sargent Rosenberg Poetry Prizes.

Raymond Soltysek has been Saltire nominated and has won a BAFTA, an RLS award and an SAC bursary. He never has enough time to do any writing though, one frustration of a career in teacher education. He is working on a textbook on behaviour management and lives at **www.soltysek.com**

Em Strang has recently completed a PhD in Creative Writing at the University of Glasgow, and is currently seeking a publisher for a first collection of poetry, *Habitude*. She teaches Creative Writing at Dumfries prison and is tutoring on the MLitt in Environment, Culture and Communication at the University of Glasgow (Dumfries).

Laura Tansley's creative and critical writing has been published in a variety of places, including *Short Fiction in Theory and Practice, Gutter* and *Kenyon Review Online* (with Micaela Maftei). She lives and works in Glasgow.

Sheila Templeton writes in both Scots and English. She has won both the McCash Scots Language and the Robert McLellan poetry competitions as well as other poetry awards. She was Makar of the Federation of Writers Scotland 2010 to 2011. Her two latest collections are *Digging for Light* New Voices Press 2011 and *Tender is the North* Red Squirrel Press 2013.

Alan Trotter is from Aberdeen and is currently studying for a PhD at the University of Glasgow. He recently completed the first draft of his novel, *Muscle*. Some other, shorter things he has written can be found at **greaterthanorequalto.net**

Hamish Whyte is a poet and editor of many anthologies of Scottish literature, including the recent *Scottish Cats* (Birlinn). He runs Mariscat Press, publishing poetry. His own latest collection is *Hannah, are you listening?* (Happenstance). He is a member of Shore Poets in Edinburgh, where he lives.